mike isabella's
crazy good italian

mike isabella's
crazy good
italian

big flavors, small plates

MIKE ISABELLA *WITH CAROL BLYMIRE*

Da Capo
LIFE
LONG

Da Capo Lifelong
A Member of the Perseus Books Group

Copyright © 2012 by Mike Isabella
Photographs © Greg Powers

Editorial production by *Marra*thon Production Services. www.marrathon.net
Designed by Lisa Diercks
Set in Abril Text and Display

Cataloging-in-Publication data for this book is available from the Library of Congress.

First Da Capo Press edition 2012
ISBN 978-0-7382-1566-2 (hardcover)
ISBN 978-0-7382-1610-2 (e-book)

Published by Da Capo Press
A Member of the Perseus Books Group
www.dacapopress.com

Da Capo Press books are available at special discounts for bulk purchases in the U.S. by corporations, institutions, and other organizations. For more information, please contact the Special Markets Department at the Perseus Books Group, 2300 Chestnut Street, Suite 200, Philadelphia, PA, 19103, or call (800) 810-4145, ext. 5000, or e-mail special.markets@perseusbooks.com.

contents

3 fresh from the farm: dairy and eggs   41

4 jersey shore style: everything fried 75

5 the family secrets: homemade italian 103

7 not your sunday macaroni   165

introduction

WHEN YOU RUN a restaurant that does 700–800 covers in a night and you want to make sure everyone gets the same great experience from start to finish, your food has to be very well thought out and easy to execute, but still pack the right balance of flavor. My food is straightforward because that's how I learned to cook, both as a kid and throughout my culinary training and restaurant cooking. It's important to me to be able to take simple ingredients and make a dish that stands out and is memorable. The recipes in this book are geared to help people cook delicious food on an everyday basis. And the food in this book? Is food I wanna eat.

I started cooking when I was five or six years old, growing up in Little Ferry, New Jersey, making meatballs with my Italian grandmother. I was a wild kid and she gave me things to do that kept me busy and out of trouble. When we went out to eat, I was always the kid trying the "weird" things on the menu. While my sister usually stuck to pasta with butter and cheese, I always wanted to order something new or different and then try to figure out how they made it.

From a really young age I knew I wanted to cook, but I didn't know what a chef was, exactly. I just wanted to be in a kitchen. As I got older, I got into trouble more often than not and the dream faded a little. When I was twenty, my grandmother passed away. Losing her shook me to the core. At the time, I was working in retail sales and barely phoning it in because I was more worried about going out every night instead of figuring out what I wanted to do with my life. My girlfriend at the time suggested I go to cooking school in New York. And since I hated my job and wanted to get my act together, I finally decided to try and get myself back on track.

My first day in class was inspiring and exciting, but I was scared. I didn't want to fail. Cooking was the only thing I truly wanted to do. I thought: *if I'm not good at this, I'm screwed.*

Fortunately, after culinary school, I got jobs in New York, Philadelphia, and Atlanta cooking with some of the best chefs and restaurateurs in those cities. My specialties became Latin, Mexican, Spanish, and Greek food, and when it came time to become an executive chef, I sent my résumé to José Andrés, who hired me to be the chef at Zaytinya in Washington, D.C. From there, I earned my own solid reviews and Zagat #1 rankings, and that opened the door to being on *Top Chef* and *Top Chef All-Stars*.

Appearing on *Top Chef All-Stars* was really important to me. I feel like the Ellis Island episode showed America the real me, not the jerk I looked like the first season I was on the show. My whole career, I had mostly avoided cooking Italian food because it was something I'd learned from my grandmother, so it didn't seem very "chef-y." But on that *All-Stars* episode, where we had to cook based on our heritage, I let my guard down and, for the first time since I made it with her as a teenager, cooked Grandma's gnocchi and gravy. It was very hard to do, and it's still hard to talk about because I really miss her and wish she were able to see what I've done with my life. I felt like she was there on the show in the kitchen with me. It was big.

As I thought about the first restaurant I wanted to open, I knew that I wanted to have the kind of restaurant where I could one day cook for my kids and share with them the flavors and experiences I had growing up. That's how the idea for Graffiato started. I didn't want to do traditional Italian food, or traditional Mediterranean food. I wanted to do *my* version of those foods I've grown to love so much. When I decided to write this cookbook, I wanted to include recipes that make the ordinary extraordinary and incorporate ingredients and flavors that give everyday home cooking that special twist. I wanted to show people how I like to cook and eat my food—big, bold flavors on small plates, with three or four different things to eat throughout the meal. Many of the recipes in the "Family Secrets" chapter serve up to six people, but most everything else is made for four people, in small portions.

In this book, you'll find recipes inspired by the cooking I did with my grandmother all the way up to the food I cook today at my restaurant and at home. These recipes are in the tradition of my family and every chef I've learned from, but at the end of the day, it's my flavors, my food. This food is who I am.

—MIKE ISABELLA

I hope this book inspires you to cook every day and try new things in the kitchen. Here are some things I want you to know before you start reading the rest of this book:

→ Always use the best ingredients you can find. It really does make a difference!

→ Make things from scratch when you can. If you can't, buy fresh and local.

→ Get to know the farmers at your farmers' market, and the other specialty food purveyors in your area. Having friendly relationships with them will only help you in the kitchen.

→ I almost exclusively use only fresh herbs in my cooking and in the recipes in this book. Cooking with fresh herbs—instead of the dried stuff in jars—is the way to go!

→ Toast and grind your own spices—a spice grinder is an inexpensive, important tool for any kitchen.

→ A Microplane is key to getting the best citrus zest and the finest shavings of hard cheese. It's a must-have for every kitchen.

→ Keep your knives sharp! If you take any cooking class, take a basic knife skills class. Learning how to hold and use a chef's knife properly will make your everyday cooking that much easier.

→ Kosher salt is your friend. Seasoning your food while you're cooking brings out the best flavor.

→ Plan ahead: read through recipes before starting to cook so you can shop accordingly and manage your time wisely. You need to give your dishes the right amount of time for flavors to set up.

→ Don't be afraid to try new things—your biggest enemy in the kitchen is fear. Be bold and try cooking and eating something new!

mike isabella's
crazy good italian

1 bites and snacks from the isabella household

WHEN MY WIFE, Stacy, and I started dating, we went out for dinner on my days off because I didn't want to cook. We enjoyed trying different restaurants in Atlanta, where we were living at the time, but as we spent more time together and got to know each other better, she decided she'd cook for me. And I let her. Every chef will tell you that when someone is willing to cook for you, you wholeheartedly say yes.

I remember her making pork ribs in a slow cooker, deviled eggs with bacon and cheese, and so many other things that made me think, "This is the right girl for me." I would eat anything she made.

In this chapter, you'll find recipes for things Stacy and I like to make on our rare days off when we have friends over to watch football or for drinks before going out. I've also included a few recipes for things you can pickle. I like pickled vegetables, especially in salads just to mix it up a bit and add a little more flavor.

In this chapter you'll also find the recipe for my famous *Pepperoni Sauce* (page 12), which I made for the *Top Chef All-Stars* finale. Not only did *Food & Wine Magazine*'s Gail Simmons rave about the sauce, calling it "crazy business," after the show was over fans and reporters kept saying, "Sorry you didn't win, but can we have the recipe for your pepperoni sauce—it sounds amazing!" At the finale the sauce was a gamble because I'd never made it before, and it turned out to be the greatest risk I ever took. I saw pepperoni in the market that day and just made up the sauce on the fly by layering tomato, fennel seed, onion, chili flakes, white wine, stock, and pepperoni. I pureed the heck out of it, and from the smell alone I *knew* I had a winner. There's a little heat, some cured sausage flavor and fennel, and it goes great with chicken thighs or wings . . . or just out of the pan with a spoon.

Pork-Fried Peanuts

These are salty, sweet, and spicy peanuts—addictive. The great thing about cooking with lard is that you can use it over and over again. After making these peanuts, just pour the melted lard through a paper towel–lined fine-mesh strainer into a jar and let it cool before storing it in the fridge.

1. On the stovetop, heat the lard in a large, heavy-bottomed pot to 350°F, using a candy thermometer to measure the temperature.

2. In a medium saucepan over high heat, bring the peanuts, water, and sugar to a boil for 5 minutes, stirring frequently, until the liquid thickens to syrup.

3. Using a slotted spoon or wok skimmer, strain the peanuts from the syrup and place them carefully into the lard. Fry at 350°F for 3 minutes, stirring occasionally.

4. Remove the peanuts from the lard and toss with orange zest, Aleppo pepper, and salt.

5. Line a baking sheet with parchment paper. Lay the peanuts evenly on the paper, making sure they don't clump together, and let them cool at room temperature for 20 minutes.

6. Break apart any peanuts that have hardened together and serve in a bowl as a party snack.

MAKES 2½–3 CUPS

ACTIVE TIME = 15 MINUTES

INACTIVE TIME = 30 MINUTES

———————★———————

4 cups lard

1 pound roasted, unsalted peanuts

2 cups water

2 cups sugar

1 tablespoon orange zest

1½ tablespoons ground Aleppo pepper (or 1 tablespoon sweet paprika plus 2 teaspoons cayenne pepper)

2 teaspoons kosher salt

Smoked Olives

MAKES 2 CUPS
ACTIVE TIME = 20 MINUTES
INACTIVE TIME = 1 HOUR, PLUS 24
HOURS MARINATING TIME

———— ★ ————

2 cups applewood chips, for the smoker or grill

2 cups mixed olives (Greek Kalamata, Moroccan oil-cured black, Italian Cerignola, Spanish Arbequina, or your favorite olives from your grocery deli)

1 cup extra virgin olive oil

Peel of ½ lemon (no pith)

Peel of ½ orange (no pith)

5 sprigs thyme

3 sprigs rosemary

1 tablespoon lemon zest

2 teaspoons coarsely chopped dill

½ teaspoon black sea salt

———— ★ ————

USE A VEGETABLE PEELER TO GET JUST THE PEEL AND NOT THE WHITE, BITTER PITH OF THE LEMON AND ORANGE IN THIS RECIPE.

These olives are a make-ahead snack—they need a day in the fridge to absorb all the flavors in the marinade. The smokiness, combined with the citrus zest, herbs, and the olive brine, will make these a favorite of yours in no time. When we make these at home, we usually do a double or triple batch because they're great to snack on throughout the week.

This recipe calls for using a smoker, but you can use a charcoal grill—just keep the heat low and don't let the olives touch the grill grate. If using a gas grill or smoker, turn off the gas right after you put the olives inside.

1. Soak the applewood chips in water for 1 hour. Prepare a smoker or grill with coals on the bottom. Once the coals are hot, place the soaked applewood chips atop the coals. Heat the smoker or grill to 200°F.

2. Place the olives in a grill basket and smoke for 15–20 minutes. Keep the smoker or grill lid closed so that the olives absorb the right amount of smoke.

3. While the olives are in the smoker, combine the olive oil, lemon peel, orange peel, thyme, and rosemary in a mixing bowl. Add the smoked olives, cover the bowl with plastic wrap, and marinate in the refrigerator for 24 hours.

4. Pour the olives and marinade through a fine-mesh strainer placed over a bowl to catch the marinade, which can be discarded or used as a marinade for chicken or shrimp.

5. Place the olives (still with the citrus peels, rosemary, and thyme) in a small mixing bowl and stir in the lemon zest and dill. Season with black sea salt and serve.

Spiced Pistachios

These spiced pistachios became such a hit with friends and family over the years that I decided to serve them at my restaurant, Graffiato. We send them out to the table so our guests have something to snack on while they're enjoying a drink and looking at the menu.

1. Preheat the oven to 400°F.

2. Blend the *Garlic Oil*, oregano, and rosemary in a blender on high speed for 2–3 minutes, until the herbs are fully incorporated.

3. Toast the fennel, coriander, and caraway seeds in a sauté pan over medium heat for 4–5 minutes, shaking the pan often to prevent burning.

4. Transfer the seeds to a spice grinder or a mini food processor, add the chili flakes, and grind to a fine powder.

5. In a mixing bowl, combine the ground seed mixture, sugar, Aleppo pepper, paprika, and salt.

6. Place the pistachios in a roasting pan. Combine the pistachios with the blended oil mixture, add the spice blend, and stir until evenly coated. Roast in the oven for 10 minutes, stirring halfway through.

MAKES APPROXIMATELY 2 CUPS
ACTIVE TIME = 25 MINUTES

———★———

¼ cup *Garlic Oil* (recipe follows)

2 teaspoons fresh oregano leaves

2 teaspoons fresh rosemary leaves

½ teaspoon fennel seeds

½ teaspoon coriander seeds

½ teaspoon caraway seeds

½ teaspoon red chili flakes

2 tablespoons sugar

½ teaspoon ground Aleppo pepper (or ¼ teaspoon ground cayenne pepper)

½ teaspoon ground smoked paprika

½ teaspoon kosher salt

1 pound roasted, salted pistachios in the shell

———★———

SPICED PISTACHIOS CAN BE STORED AT ROOM TEMPERATURE FOR 3 DAYS.

Garlic Oil

1. Heat the olive oil and garlic in a small saucepan over medium heat for 5 minutes, stirring to make sure the garlic cloves are coated in oil. Lower the heat to keep warm for an additional 35–40 minutes, moving the garlic around the pan every so often to prevent burning.

2. Let the oil and garlic cool to room temperature. Store, covered, in the refrigerator up to 30 days.

MAKES 1½ CUPS
ACTIVE TIME = 45 MINUTES

———★———

1½ cups extra virgin olive oil

6 garlic cloves, peeled

———★———

DO NOT DISCARD THE GARLIC CLOVES. THEY ARE JUST LIKE ROASTED GARLIC AND CAN BE USED IN RECIPES OR SPREAD ON TOAST.

Spicy Popcorn

MAKES 10–12 CUPS, POPPED

ACTIVE TIME = 10 MINUTES

——————★——————

2 tablespoons canola oil

½ cup popcorn kernels (white Amish recommended)

4 tablespoons unsalted butter

2 teaspoons minced garlic

¼ cup grated Parmigiano-Reggiano

1½ tablespoons red chili flakes

1 tablespoon dried oregano

1½ teaspoons kosher salt

——————★——————

SEE PHOTOGRAPH, FACING PAGE 1

There's nothing like the smell of real popcorn popping—not the microwave kind. This snack is really easy to make and hopefully will inspire you to try your own flavor combinations. You'll never go back to the stuff in the envelope. This is the real deal.

1. Pour the canola oil into a large saucepan on the stovetop. Add the popcorn kernels and cover with a tight-fitting lid.

2. Turn the heat to high. When the kernels begin to pop, shake the pan every 30 seconds—keeping the lid on—so that the popcorn doesn't burn. When the kernels stop popping (after about 2 or 3 minutes), remove from heat.

3. Melt the butter in a small saucepan over medium heat. Add the garlic and stir frequently for 3–4 minutes, until the garlic turns golden brown.

4. Pour the garlic butter through a fine-mesh strainer into a small bowl and discard garlic.

5. Grind the Parmigiano-Reggiano, chili flakes, oregano, and salt in a spice grinder until the mixture looks like sand.

6. Toss the popcorn with the garlic butter and cheese mixture until the popcorn is evenly seasoned.

Olive Oil–Fried Chips

These chips are best eaten right after you make them. They'll be good for about a day, but they're best when warm, just out of the fryer. Make sure your vegetables are all the same size, 2–3 inches in diameter, so they'll cook evenly, and season them as soon as they come out of the oil so the salt and pepper cling to the chips.

MAKES 6–8 CUPS CHIPS
ACTIVE TIME = 45 MINUTES

———— ★ ————

6 cups canola oil

2 cups extra virgin olive oil

1 Yukon gold potato

1 sweet potato

1 purple potato

1 golden beet

1 red beet

1 tablespoon sea salt (or to taste)

2 teaspoons finely ground black pepper (or to taste)

1. Heat the oils in an electric deep fryer to 325°F. If you do not have a deep fryer, use a heavy-bottomed pot with a candy thermometer clipped to the inside.

2. Wash, but do not peel, the vegetables.

3. Have ready two bowls of cold water. Using a mandoline, thinly slice each vegetable into 1/16-inch slices. Keep the slices in cold water while you slice the other vegetables, keeping the red beet slices in a separate bowl so they don't "bleed" onto the other vegetables.

4. Before frying, thoroughly pat the sliced vegetables dry with paper towels or a dish towel. This is a very important step, as you do not want any water in the hot oil.

5. Line a baking sheet with paper towels.

6. Fry the vegetables in small batches (don't overcrowd them or they won't cook evenly) until crispy, approximately 1½–2 minutes per batch. Use a slotted spoon or wok skimmer to remove them from the oil and drain on the baking sheet. (Make sure the oil temperature stays consistent between batches to ensure even cooking.) Immediately season the chips with sea salt and pepper.

Chicken Wings with Pepperoni Sauce

MAKES APPROXIMATELY 1½ CUPS

ACTIVE TIME = 1 HOUR, 20 MINUTES

———————★———————

PEPPERONI SAUCE

1 tablespoon extra virgin olive oil

¼ cup diced yellow onion

1 garlic clove, thinly sliced

6 ounces pepperoni, thinly sliced

½ teaspoon fennel seed

½ teaspoon red chili flakes

½ cup canned crushed tomatoes

1½ cups chicken broth or stock

½ teaspoon red wine vinegar

———————★———————

PEPPERONI SAUCE CAN BE REFRIGERATED FOR UP TO 3 DAYS OR FROZEN FOR UP TO 3 MONTHS. REHEAT THE SAUCE BEFORE YOU ARE READY TO USE.

You can't write a book called Crazy Good Italian *without including pepperoni. I serve this sauce with chicken thighs or flatbread at Graffiato—it's our #1 seller. Here, I use chicken wings because I think they make a better snack. They're also affordable, as are all the ingredients in this recipe. This dish is proof that you don't have to be a fancy chef to create something flavorful and memorable for your friends and family.*

Pepperoni Sauce

1. Heat the olive oil in a large saucepan over medium heat. Add the onion and garlic and sweat for 4–5 minutes until soft and translucent. If the garlic begins to brown, lower the heat.

2. Add the pepperoni and sauté for 4 minutes. Meanwhile, in a separate dry sauté pan, toast the fennel seed over medium heat for 2–3 minutes, shaking the pan often to prevent burning. Add the chili flakes and toast 1 minute longer, then add the toasted spices to the pepperoni mixture.

3. Stir in the crushed tomatoes and simmer for 3 minutes. Add the chicken broth and increase heat to bring to a gentle boil. Lower the heat and simmer for 50 minutes, stirring every now and then.

4. Remove from heat and let cool slightly. Transfer the

mixture to a blender and purée for 2–3 minutes or until smooth.

5. Pass the sauce through a fine-mesh strainer into a mixing bowl, using the back of a spoon or a silicone spatula to help the sauce pass through.

6. Finish the sauce by stirring in the red wine vinegar.

Chicken Wings

1. Using a sharp knife, remove and discard the chicken wing tips. Then, cut each wing into two pieces: find the joint and cut at the joint to separate the drumette from the wing.

2. In a large glass mixing bowl or other nonreactive bowl, combine the olive oil, garlic, rosemary, and lemon peel. Add the chicken wings and stir until well coated. Cover the bowl with plastic wrap and marinate in the refrigerator for 2½ hours.

3. Preheat the oven to 450°F. Remove the wings from the refrigerator and let rest at room temperature for 10 minutes. Stir in the salt.

4. Place wings on a baking rack on top of a baking sheet to allow for even cooking. Don't rinse the marinade from the wings, but do make sure there's no garlic, rosemary, or lemon peel on the chicken—they will burn.

5. Roast the wings for 25–30 minutes, until golden brown and crispy.

6. Pour ¾ cup warm *Pepperoni Sauce* into a large mixing bowl, add the wings, and toss to coat. Transfer wings to a serving platter and serve the remaining sauce on the side.

SERVES 4 AS A SMALL PLATE

ACTIVE TIME = 40 MINUTES

INACTIVE TIME = 2 HOURS, 30 MINUTES

———————★———————

CHICKEN WINGS

8 whole chicken wings (about 2½ pounds)

3 tablespoons extra virgin olive oil

3 garlic cloves, smashed

2 sprigs rosemary

Peel of 1 lemon (no pith)

½ teaspoon kosher salt

1½ cups *Pepperoni Sauce* (previous page)

Deviled Bacon, Egg, and Cheese

MAKES 12 SERVINGS

ACTIVE TIME = 35 MINUTES

———————★———————

6 large eggs

4 slices thick-cut bacon, rough chopped into ¼-inch pieces

3 tablespoons sour cream

½ teaspoon yellow mustard

½ cup finely shredded sharp Cheddar (white Vermont recommended)

3 teaspoons finely diced chives

Kosher salt to taste

My wife, Stacy, knows how much deviled eggs remind me of home, so she created this recipe to bring together two of my favorite comfort foods: deviled eggs and a bacon cheeseburger (minus the burger part). She makes these eggs every year for July 4th, and they're usually gone before our friends even make it over to our house for pre-fireworks drinks and dinner. That's how good they are. You get a nice sharp cheddar flavor, and the crunchy bacon on top makes it smoky.

1. Place the eggs in a medium saucepan and cover with cold water, keeping an inch of water above the eggs. Bring to a rolling boil and cover the pan. Remove from heat, keep covered, and let eggs rest in the hot water for 12 minutes.

2. In a nonstick pan, sauté the bacon over medium-high heat until crispy. Drain on a paper towel–lined plate and mince until crumb-like.

3. Drain the eggs and place them in a bowl under cold running water for 3 minutes. Peel the eggs and slice them in half lengthwise.

4. Separate the yolks from the whites. Place yolks in a medium-size mixing bowl, smash them with a fork, and stir in the sour cream and mustard. Mix until smooth.

5. Add the bacon (reserving 1 teaspoon for garnish), Cheddar, and 2 teaspoons chives to the yolk mixture, stirring to fully incorporate.

6. Taste to determine if salt is needed. Salt content in bacon varies, so it's best to use your own judgment. Season with salt as desired.

7. Put the mixture in a piping bag (or Ziploc bag with a corner snipped off) and fill each egg white half.

8. Refrigerate until ready to serve. Before serving, garnish the deviled eggs with the remaining chives and bacon.

In a Pickle

I like to add pickled elements to much of the food I make at home and in my restaurants. Here are some recipes for things you can pickle and snack on, serve with cheese and charcuterie, or throw into a salad to brighten it up. Pickling is easy to do—don't be intimidated by it. When it comes to equipment, you don't need anything special: just a few clean Mason or Ball glass jars and lids. You can clean your jars and lids by running them through the hottest cycle possible in your dishwasher.

Pickled Feta

ACTIVE TIME = 15 MINUTES
INACTIVE TIME = 30 MINUTES, PLUS
1 WEEK PICKLING TIME

———————★———————

1 cup cold water

½ cup sugar

¼ cup red wine (Cabernet Sauvignon recommended)

¼ cup red wine vinegar

½ pound feta cheese block, cut into 1-inch cubes

1. In a small saucepan, bring the water, sugar, wine, and vinegar to a boil over high heat, stirring to dissolve the sugar.

2. Remove from heat and transfer to heatproof bowl. Refrigerate for 30 minutes. It's important to let the pickling brine cool in the fridge so it won't melt the feta.

3. Place the feta cubes in a large glass jar. Pour the chilled liquid over them, seal the jar with a tight-fitting lid, and refrigerate for 1 week.

CAN BE REFRIGERATED UP TO 1 MONTH.

Pickled Cherry Tomatoes

ACTIVE TIME = 30 MINUTES
INACTIVE TIME = 1 HOUR, PLUS
1 WEEK PICKLING TIME

———————★———————

1 pound cherry tomatoes

1 teaspoon black peppercorns

½ teaspoon whole allspice

2 cloves

1 cinnamon stick

1 star anise (optional)

1½ cups cold water

1 cup champagne vinegar

½ cup sugar

1. Bring a large pot of water to a boil. Set a bowl of ice water to the side.

2. Score the cherry tomatoes on the stem end by making an "X" with a paring knife. To loosen the skins, blanch the tomatoes for 30–45 seconds and shock in ice water. Remove and discard skins.

3. In a dry sauté pan, toast the peppercorns, allspice, cloves, cinnamon stick, and star anise over medium heat for 5 minutes, shaking the pan often to prevent burning.

4. In a small saucepan, bring the water, vinegar, sugar, and toasted peppercorns, allspice, cloves, cinnamon stick, and star anise to a boil over high heat, stirring to dissolve the sugar.

5. Place the tomatoes in a large glass jar. Pour the hot liquid over them into the jar, leave the jar uncovered, and let rest at room temperature for 1 hour. Seal the jar with a tight-fitting lid and refrigerate for 1 week before using.

CAN BE REFRIGERATED UP TO 1 MONTH.

Pickled Kumquats

ACTIVE TIME = 15 MINUTES
INACTIVE TIME = 1 HOUR, PLUS
24 HOURS PICKLING TIME

———————★———————

1 tablespoon coriander seed

3 cardamom pods

1 cinnamon stick

1½ cups cold water

½ cup white wine vinegar

½ cup orange juice

½ cup sugar

1 pound kumquats, sliced into ¼-inch rings

1. In a dry sauté pan, toast the coriander, cardamom, and cinnamon stick over medium heat for 5 minutes, shaking the pan frequently to prevent burning.

2. In a small saucepan, bring the water, vinegar, orange juice, sugar, sliced kumquats, and toasted coriander, cardamom, and cinnamon stick to a boil over high heat. Lower the heat and simmer for 5 minutes.

3. Transfer the mixture to a large glass jar and let rest at room temperature for 1 hour. Seal the jar with a tight-fitting lid and refrigerate for 24 hours.

CAN BE REFRIGERATED UP TO 3 MONTHS.

Pickled Champagne Grapes

ACTIVE TIME = 15 MINUTES
INACTIVE TIME = 1 HOUR, PLUS
1 WEEK PICKLING TIME

———————★———————

5 whole cloves

2 teaspoons coriander seed

1 teaspoon black peppercorns

1½ cups cold water

1 cup champagne vinegar

½ cup sugar

5 slices fresh ginger (⅛-inch thick)

1 pound champagne grapes

1. In a dry sauté pan, toast the cloves, coriander, and black peppercorns over medium heat for 5 minutes, shaking the pan often to prevent burning. Remove from heat.

2. In a small saucepan, bring the water, vinegar, sugar, ginger, and toasted cloves, coriander seeds, and peppercorns to a boil over high heat, stirring to dissolve the sugar.

3. Place the champagne grapes in a large glass jar. Pour the hot liquid over them into the jar, leave the jar uncovered, and let rest at room temperature for 1 hour. Seal the jar with a tight-fitting lid and refrigerate for 1 week before using.

CAN BE REFRIGERATED UP TO 6 MONTHS.

Pickled Red Pearl Onions

ACTIVE TIME = 15 MINUTES
INACTIVE TIME = 1 HOUR

———★———

1½ cups cold water

1 cup red wine vinegar

½ cup sugar

1 pound red pearl onions, peeled

1. In a medium saucepan, bring the water, vinegar, sugar, and onions to a boil over high heat, stirring to dissolve the sugar. Lower the heat and simmer for 5 minutes.

2. Transfer the mixture to a large glass jar, leave the jar uncovered, and let rest at room temperature for 1 hour. Seal the jar with a tight-fitting lid and refrigerate.

THE PICKLED ONIONS CAN BE EATEN RIGHT AWAY, AND CAN BE REFRIGERATED UP TO 6 MONTHS.

Pickled Sunchokes

ACTIVE TIME = 15 MINUTES
INACTIVE TIME = 1 HOUR

———★———

1 tablespoon dried yellow mustard seeds

1 teaspoon celery seeds

1½ cups cold water

1 cup white wine vinegar

½ cup sugar

½ pound sunchokes, scrubbed clean and thinly sliced using a mandoline

1. Toast the mustard seeds and celery seeds in a dry sauté pan over medium heat for 5 minutes, shaking the pan frequently to prevent burning.

2. In a small saucepan, bring the water, vinegar, sugar, mustard seeds, and celery seeds to a boil over high heat, stirring to dissolve the sugar.

3. Place the sunchoke slices in a large glass jar. Pour the hot liquid over them, leave the jar uncovered, and let rest at room temperature for 1 hour. Seal the jar with a tight-fitting lid and refrigerate.

THE PICKLED SUNCHOKES CAN BE EATEN AFTER 1 HOUR IN THE REFRIGERATOR AND CAN BE REFRIGERATED UP TO 6 MONTHS.

———★———

SUNCHOKES ARE ALSO SOMETIMES CALLED JERUSALEM ARTICHOKES.

2 vegetate

I LIKE TO THINK of the vegetable dishes in this chapter as *antipasti*, meaning you serve them as a starter before the main course. Or, you can do what my mom did when I was growing up—put a few plates of vegetables on the dinner table with some cheese and pesto, and a loaf of crusty Italian bread, and just go to town. It's a different way of thinking about dinner. You don't need the traditional meat, starch, and a vegetable to make a meal—you can do a bunch of small plates, like I suggest throughout this book. Have fun with it and be creative!

In this chapter, I've included recipes for vegetables that span all the seasons of the year. To me, there's nothing better than going to the farmers' market and seeing the season's bounty spread out across the market stalls. Squash and leafy greens in the fall . . . root vegetables in the winter . . . peas and carrots in the spring . . . corn and tomatoes in the summer. Sometimes, it can be sensory overload, but in a good way. A really good way.

My mom was a vegetarian and I used to complain about that when I was a kid, but I look back on it now and realize how her inventiveness with vegetables throughout the year inspires me today. I love cooking pork, lamb, and other meat, but I also love the challenge of creating a plate of vegetables that doesn't feel like an afterthought. These vegetable recipes really shine and bolster the goodness that's inherent in every season's offerings.

Blistered Sweet Peppers

SERVES 4 AS A SMALL PLATE

ACTIVE TIME = 1 HOUR, 10 MINUTES

INACTIVE TIME = 20 MINUTES

———————— ★ ————————

3 red bell peppers, brushed with extra virgin olive oil and seasoned with salt

3 yellow bell peppers, brushed with extra virgin olive oil and seasoned with salt

¼ cup extra virgin olive oil

½ cup thinly sliced red onion

2 tablespoons minced garlic

¼ teaspoon red chili flakes

¼ teaspoon paprika

4 whole pickled peppadew peppers, finely diced

1 bay leaf

1 sprig rosemary

1 sprig thyme

1 tablespoon red wine vinegar

1 tablespoon capers

½ teaspoon kosher salt

Though they're best in-season in the summer, you can find bell peppers year-round in the grocery store, so this dish kind of transcends all seasons. Peppers and onions are a classic Italian pairing; here, I've also included pickled sweet peppers and capers to brighten the dish with some acid and give it more depth of flavor.

1. Preheat the oven broiler on high. Place the oven rack in the second-highest position.

2. Place the whole red and yellow bell peppers on their sides on a baking sheet and broil for 5 minutes on each side, leaving about 3 inches between the top of the peppers and the broiler flame. This will take 20–25 minutes. The skins will become charred and the flesh soft.

3. Place the peppers in a glass bowl and cover tightly with plastic wrap. Let cool at room temperature for 20 minutes.

4. Slice the cooled peppers lengthwise in half and remove and discard the skin, ribs, and seeds. Slice into ¼-inch strips and set aside.

5. Heat the olive oil in a large saucepan over medium heat and sweat the onions for 5 minutes or until soft and translucent. Add the garlic and sauté for 2 minutes.

6. Stir in the chili flakes and paprika, then add the roasted pepper strips, peppadews, bay leaf, rosemary,

and thyme. Lower heat and cook at a low simmer for 20 minutes to allow flavors to come together.

7. Stir in the red wine vinegar and capers and simmer for 5 minutes. Remove and discard bay leaf, rosemary, and thyme. Stir in the salt.

8. Transfer to a serving bowl and serve at room temperature.

———★———

YOU CAN FIND PICKLED PEPPADEW PEPPERS WITH THE PICKLES AND RELISHES AT YOUR LOCAL GROCERY STORE. IF YOUR STORE HAS AN OLIVE BAR, CHECK THERE, TOO!

———★———

Broccolini with Roasted Pepper Relish and Feta

Broccolini is a hybrid of broccoli and Chinese kale. I like it because the stalks are long and tender and the florets are smaller than broccoli, which means it needs less time to cook. Because it's more mellow in flavor than broccoli, you can use it with a wider variety of ingredients to make a great vegetable dish.

1. In a stockpot, bring the water and salt to a boil. Set a bowl of ice water to the side.

2. Trim 1 inch from the end of each broccolini stem and discard. Blanch the broccolini for 1 minute and shock in ice water until chilled. Pat dry with paper towels.

3. Arrange broccolini on a serving dish and top with the *Roasted Pepper Relish* and feta. Serve at room temperature.

SERVES 4 AS A SMALL PLATE
ACTIVE TIME = 15 MINUTES

———★———

4 quarts water

2 tablespoons kosher salt

16 stalks broccolini

1 cup *Roasted Pepper Relish* (recipe follows)

½ cup crumbled feta

———★———

PICKLED PEPPADEW PEPPERS ARE ONE OF MY FAVORITE CONDIMENTS. OPEN MY REFRIGERATOR, AND YOU'LL ALWAYS SEE THEM IN THERE. THEY'RE SWEET WITH JUST A MILD HIT OF HEAT.

Roasted Pepper Relish

If you're short on time, ¾ cup finely diced jarred roasted red peppers can be substituted for roasting your own bell peppers.

MAKES APPROXIMATELY 1 CUP
ACTIVE TIME = 35–40 MINUTES
INACTIVE TIME = 20 MINUTES

———————★———————

2 red bell peppers, brushed with extra virgin olive oil and seasoned with salt

½ cup chopped walnuts

3 pickled peppadew peppers, finely chopped

1 pickled red cherry pepper, stem and seeds removed, finely chopped

¼ cup extra virgin olive oil

1 tablespoon red wine vinegar

½ teaspoon kosher salt

———————★———————

RELISH CAN BE REFRIGERATED FOR 1 WEEK.

1. Preheat the broiler on high. Place the oven rack in the second-highest position.

2. Place the bell peppers on their sides on a baking sheet and broil for 5 minutes on each side, leaving about 3 inches between the top of the peppers and the broiler flame. This will take 20–25 minutes. The skins will become charred and the flesh soft.

3. Place the peppers in a glass bowl and cover tightly with plastic wrap. Let cool at room temperature for 20 minutes.

4. In a dry sauté pan, toast the walnuts over medium heat for 7–8 minutes, shaking the pan often to prevent burning. When the walnuts are fragrant and toasted, remove from heat and finely chop.

5. Slice the cooled peppers lengthwise in half and remove the skin, ribs, and seeds. Finely dice, place in a bowl, and toss with walnuts, peppadews, red cherry pepper, olive oil, red wine vinegar, and salt.

———

Arugula Insalata

I like a little sweet and salt balance in my salads, with a big, bold vinaigrette. Pickled kumquats or sunchokes work really well with the peppery arugula, and the grapes add a hint of sweetness. I top a lot of my salads with ricotta salata—it just works for me.

1. Combine arugula, grapes, and your choice of pickled item in a salad bowl.

2. In a separate small mixing bowl, whisk together olive oil, vinegar, and salt and drizzle over arugula, tossing together to evenly coat.

3. Top with ricotta salata and serve immediately.

SERVES 4 AS A SMALL PLATE

ACTIVE TIME = 5 MINUTES

———★———

3 ounces baby arugula

1 cup red seedless grapes, halved

½ cup *Pickled Kumquats* or ½ cup *Pickled Sunchokes* (see recipes on pages 18 and 19)

2 tablespoons extra virgin olive oil

1 tablespoon white balsamic vinegar

¼ teaspoon kosher salt

⅓ cup crumbled ricotta salata

Brussels Sprouts with Pancetta and Maple Glaze

When the weather gets colder, I look forward to making Brussels sprouts. I didn't really like eating them until I figured out how to make them sweet and salty. The sweet maple glaze complements the saltiness of the pancetta and brings out the great cabbage flavor in the sprouts.

1. Preheat the oven to 475°F.

2. Heat 2 teaspoons olive oil in a medium saucepan over medium-high heat. Add the pancetta and sauté for 8–10 minutes, or until the fat has rendered and the pancetta is crispy. Add the shallot and sauté 2 minutes longer.

3. Stir in sherry vinegar, maple syrup, and brown sugar. Bring to a boil, then lower heat to medium and simmer to reduce the liquid by half. This will take 20–25 minutes.

4. While the maple glaze is reducing, toss the Brussels sprouts with remaining 3 tablespoons olive oil and salt. Stir to evenly coat and season the Brussels sprouts. Arrange them on a baking sheet in a single layer and roast for 20–25 minutes.

5. Toss Brussels sprouts with maple glaze, transfer to a serving dish, and serve hot.

SERVES 4 AS A SMALL PLATE
ACTIVE TIME = 35–40 MINUTES

———————★———————

2 teaspoons plus 3 tablespoons extra virgin olive oil

1 cup small-diced pancetta (approximately 4 ounces)

½ cup small-diced shallot

¾ cup sherry vinegar

¾ cup maple syrup

¼ cup light brown sugar

1 pound Brussels sprouts, quartered

1 teaspoon kosher salt

Shaved Fennel with Peaches and Hazelnuts

SERVES 4 AS A SMALL PLATE

ACTIVE TIME = 30–35 MINUTES

———————★———————

2 whole peaches

2 tablespoons extra virgin olive oil

¼ teaspoon plus ¼ teaspoon kosher salt

½ cup whole hazelnuts

2 tablespoons canola oil

1 tablespoon champagne vinegar

2 cups thinly shaved fennel (use a mandoline)

1 tablespoon finely chopped fennel fronds

Every year, I look forward to stone fruit season in the summer. Peaches, nectarines, plums . . . they're some of my favorite fruits. In this dish, I like the way the anise flavor of the fennel balances the sweet, juicy peach. Hazelnuts add great crunchy texture and expand the overall flavor of every bite.

1. Preheat the oven to 375°F.

2. Quarter the peaches and discard the pit. Toss in a bowl with 1 tablespoon olive oil and ¼ teaspoon salt. Place flesh side up on a baking sheet and roast for 15 minutes.

3. Place the hazelnuts on a separate baking sheet and roast for 10–12 minutes or until fragrant. Remove from the oven and rub off and discard as much remaining dark brown skin as you can. Roughly chop the hazelnuts and set aside.

4. Allow the peaches to cool to the touch. Remove and discard the skin from two of the peach quarters. Place them in a blender with canola oil, champagne vinegar, remaining ¼ teaspoon salt, and remaining 1 tablespoon olive oil and blend on medium for 45–60 seconds, until a smooth vinaigrette forms.

5. Peel and slice the other roast peach quarters into ⅛-inch slices. Toss the peaches, shaved fennel, and fennel fronds with the peach vinaigrette. Transfer to a large serving dish and top with roasted hazelnuts.

Marinated Baby Bellos

SERVES 4 AS A SMALL PLATE

ACTIVE TIME = 30 MINUTES

———— ★ ————

1½ pounds baby portobello mushrooms

3 tablespoons plus 3 tablespoons extra virgin olive oil

½ teaspoon plus ½ teaspoon salt

2 tablespoons red wine vinegar

1 teaspoon Dijon mustard

1 teaspoon honey

2 tablespoons *Pickled Mustard Seeds* (recipe follows)

1 tablespoon small-diced cherry peppers (found in the olive and relish aisle of your grocery store)

1 tablespoon finely chopped parsley

———— ★ ————

THE MARINATED MUSHROOMS CAN BE KEPT IN THE REFRIGERATOR FOR 1 WEEK.

You can eat these marinated mushrooms on their own. They're tangy and sweet and would be great served with cheese and a plate of ham or salami. Or toss them in pasta with some really good olive oil, slice them and use as a pizza topping, or serve them over polenta.

1. Preheat the oven to 375°F.

2. Wipe any dirt from the mushrooms with a damp paper towel. Remove and discard stems. Cut the caps into quarters.

3. Toss mushrooms with 3 tablespoons olive oil and ½ teaspoon salt. Place on a baking sheet in a single layer and roast for 15 minutes, stirring halfway through the cooking time to ensure they roast evenly.

4. In a bowl, whisk together the red wine vinegar, mustard, honey, and remaining salt. Slowly stream in the remaining olive oil while continuing to whisk, to emulsify it and form a vinaigrette.

5. Stir in *Pickled Mustard Seeds*, cherry peppers, and parsley.

6. Add the roasted mushrooms (and any liquid they may have released) while they're still warm to the vinaigrette. Stir to coat and serve at room temperature.

Pickled Mustard Seeds

1. In a small saucepan, bring the mustard seeds and 2 cups water to a boil over high heat for 5 minutes.

2. Strain and rinse mustard seeds in a fine-mesh strainer under cold, running water. Transfer them to a heat-resistant bowl.

3. In a small saucepan, bring sugar, vinegar, and ¼ cup water to a boil over high heat, stirring to dissolve the sugar.

4. Pour the boiling mixture over the mustard seeds. Let them rest at room temperature for at least 1 hour, but no more than 24 hours.

5. Strain the mustard seeds, discarding the liquid, and store, covered, in the refrigerator.

MAKES ¼ CUP

ACTIVE TIME = 15–20 MINUTES

INACTIVE TIME = 1 HOUR

———————★———————

2 tablespoons dried yellow mustard seeds

2 cups plus ¼ cup cold water

2 tablespoons sugar

¼ cup white vinegar

———————★———————

CAN BE STORED IN THE REFRIGERATOR FOR 1 WEEK.

Roasted Cauliflower with Pecorino and Mint

SERVES 4 AS A SMALL PLATE

ACTIVE TIME = 25 MINUTES

———— ★ ————

4 tablespoons unsalted butter

1 small head cauliflower, cut into florets (approximately 4–5 cups)

½ teaspoon kosher salt

½ cup thinly shaved red onion

¼ cup grated Pecorino

10 mint leaves, rolled and thinly sliced (chiffonade)

1 tablespoon lemon juice

Kosher salt, to taste

———— ★ ————

IT IS IMPORTANT TO USE A STAINLESS STEEL PAN WHEN MAKING THE BROWN BUTTER, SO YOU CAN SEE THE BUTTER CHANGE COLOR.

Roasting cauliflower is one of the easiest ways to prepare this heady vegetable, and the brown butter and Pecorino only make it taste more nutty and hearty. The onions bring a needed acidity to lighten and open up the cauliflower flavor, and the mint brightens every bite.

1. Preheat the oven to 500°F.

2. In a stainless steel sauté pan, melt the butter over medium heat, whisking to ensure it doesn't burn. You will start to see little brown bits begin to form. Keep whisking until the butter turns light brown and has a nutty aroma. Remove from heat.

3. In a large glass mixing bowl, toss the cauliflower florets with the brown butter and salt, then transfer to a baking sheet and roast for 15 minutes or until just tender.

4. In a large mixing bowl, toss the hot cauliflower with the red onion, Pecorino, and mint. Drizzle lemon juice over the cauliflower and season with more kosher salt to taste.

5. Transfer to a serving dish and serve hot.

Snap Peas with Goat Cheese and Tomato Pesto

SERVES 4 AS A SMALL PLATE

ACTIVE TIME = 20 MINUTES

———— ★ ————

4 quarts water

2 tablespoons plus ¼ teaspoon kosher salt

¾ pound snap peas (in pods)

1 tablespoon extra virgin olive oil

Zest of ½ lemon

1 teaspoon sesame seeds

¼ cup *Tomato Pesto* (recipe follows)

2 ounces goat cheese, crumbled

Blanching and shocking vegetables not only preserves nutrients, it also enhances their flavor and visual appeal. These peas are a fresh, bright green, and the tomato pesto and goat cheese bring creaminess and vivid contrast to this dish.

1. In a large saucepan or stockpot, bring the water and 2 tablespoons of salt to a boil. Set a bowl of ice water to the side.

2. Remove the peapod strings by tugging at the tip of each snap pea and pulling it down the back of the pod. Cut off the stem ends and leave pods whole.

3. Blanch the peas for one minute and shock in ice water until chilled. Pat dry with paper towels.

4. Toss snap peas, olive oil, lemon zest, and remaining ¼ teaspoon salt in a mixing bowl. Let rest at room temperature.

5. In a small dry sauté pan, toast the sesame seeds over medium heat for 5 minutes, shaking pan often to prevent burning.

6. Transfer snap peas to a serving bowl and top with dollops of *Tomato Pesto* and goat cheese. Garnish with toasted sesame seeds. Serve at room temperature.

Tomato Pesto

Three tablespoons finely diced jarred roasted red peppers can be substituted for roasting your own.

1. Preheat the oven broiler on high. Place the oven rack in the second-highest position.

2. Toss the whole tomatoes and pepper with 2 teaspoons olive oil and ½ teaspoon salt. Place on a baking sheet and broil on all sides, 5 minutes on each side, leaving about 3 inches between the top of the peppers and the broiler flame. This will take 20–25 minutes.

3. Place the broiled tomatoes and pepper in a glass bowl and cover tightly with plastic wrap, allowing it to cool for 20 minutes.

4. Meanwhile, in a dry sauté pan, toast the almonds over medium heat for 3 minutes, shaking the pan often to prevent burning.

5. Slice cooled pepper in half and remove the skin, seeds, and ribs. Rough-chop one-half of the pepper. Save the other half for another recipe or to snack on.

6. Place the tomatoes, garlic, almonds, and chopped pepper in a food processor. Pulse while slowly drizzling in the remaining olive oil, for 1–2 minutes, or until chunky.

7. Transfer the pesto to a bowl and stir in lemon juice, Thai basil, parsley, and remaining ½ teaspoon salt.

MAKES 1 CUP

ACTIVE TIME = 45 MINUTES

————★————

3 plum tomatoes

1 red bell pepper

2 teaspoons plus ¼ cup extra virgin olive oil

½ teaspoon plus ½ teaspoon kosher salt

¼ cup slivered almonds

2 cloves *Roasted Garlic* (page 62)

2 tablespoons lemon juice

1 tablespoon finely chopped Thai basil

1 tablespoon finely chopped parsley

————★————

PESTO CAN BE REFRIGERATED FOR 3 DAYS.

Spiced Beets with Almonds, Orange, and Arugula

SERVES 4 AS A SMALL PLATE

ACTIVE TIME = 25 MINUTES

INACTIVE TIME = 50 MINUTES

——————★——————

2 tablespoons black peppercorns

2 tablespoons whole allspice

2 tablespoons coriander seeds

1 tablespoon dried juniper berries

2 cinnamon sticks

2 star anise

Peel of 1 orange (no pith) plus supremed segments and juice

Peel of 1 lemon (no pith)

2 pounds red beets (medium-size, greens removed, scrubbed clean)

3 tablespoons extra virgin olive oil

2 teaspoons kosher salt

2 teaspoons orange juice

½ cup roasted, salted Marcona almonds

½ cup loosely packed baby arugula

Roasting beets with aromatics enhances their flavor and pulls in the warmth the spices provide. Marcona almonds give this dish a nice, salty crunch, and the citrus peel brightens it all up. This dish would go well with pork, because the flavors will complement each other.

1. Preheat oven to 325°F.

2. In a dry sauté pan, toast the peppercorns, allspice, coriander, juniper berries, cinnamon sticks, and star anise over medium heat for 5 minutes, shaking the pan often to prevent burning. Place toasted, fragrant spices in a 9 x 13-inch baking dish and add the orange and lemon peels.

3. Toss beets in 2 tablespoons olive oil and the salt and place in the baking dish atop the spices. Cover with a sheet of parchment paper, then cover the baking dish tightly with aluminum foil.

4. Roast for 50 minutes or until beets are tender. Use a cake tester to check doneness; when it slides out easily, the beets are done.

5. Uncover the dish to allow beets to cool slightly to the touch. Use a paper towel to wipe the skin from the beets.

6. Slice each orange supreme into thirds.

7. Slice beets into ½-inch x 2-inch sticks. Gently toss beets with remaining olive oil, orange segments, orange juice, and Marcona almonds.

8. Transfer to a serving bowl and top with arugula. Serve at room temperature.

How to Supreme an Orange

When you supreme an orange (or a grapefruit), you are removing the peel and the white membrane that encases the segments. This allows you to work with and enjoy the pure pulp and flavor.

→ Using a sharp paring knife or 6-inch chef's knife, slice off the top and bottom of the orange, exposing the pulp.

→ Starting at the top where the pith meets the pulp, slice down the sides of the orange, following the curve of the fruit, to remove the peel and pith. This will leave you with an orange ball.

→ Cup the orange in your hand and place your knife as close to the white membrane as you can. Slice down toward the core of the orange so that you cut out the orange segments in wedges.

→ Remove each supreme, which should have no membrane at all—just an intact, juicy segment of orange.

3 fresh from the farm: dairy and eggs

THESE DAYS, CHEFS aren't the only ones who have access to the best local ingredients—so do you. Scout out the farmers' markets where you live. It might take a little time, but once you do, it will change for the better the way you cook and eat.

There is such simplicity in using the freshest ingredients, and it makes your food taste that much better. Supporting local farms and local purveyors is something I think is really important to do. And, if you take the time to get to know the farmers who come to your local markets, they will keep you in mind when they've got something new or have something extra-special on hand.

In this chapter, I'm focusing on sources of protein and calcium that taste really, really good—I'm talking eggs and cheese. Fresh eggs, pulled from the chicken coop that morning or just days before, are like nothing else. If the chickens roam and feed off the land, the yolks of their eggs will be a deep, dark golden yellow or orange, and they'll sit up high when you crack the egg open into a bowl or sauté pan. Eggs are inexpensive, nutritious, and can be prepared so many different ways. I have two different poached egg recipes in this book, because there are few things in this world that can't be made better with a poached egg on top.

This chapter will also show you how simple it is to make your own cheese. I make my own cheese at my restaurant, Graffiato, and we use fresh milk and cream from a local dairy. When making the mozzarella, burrata, and ricotta in this book, be sure to use good, fresh milk and cream. Believe me, you'll be able to taste the difference, and you'll never want to eat store-bought cheese again.

Homemade Ricotta

Whether you need ricotta for one of my recipes or in a dish of your own, I hope you'll take the time to make fresh, homemade ricotta. It's probably the easiest cheese in the world to make. You'll need cheesecloth, but if you can't find it or you've run out, you can MacGyver a coffee filter to do the cheesecloth's job. You can find cheesecloth in most grocery stores, large department stores, or kitchen goods stores.

1. Tie the thyme, bay leaf, and lemon peel into a bundle with kitchen twine.

2. In a large saucepan or stockpot, combine the milk, salt, and herb bundle and cook over medium-high heat. Stir in the citric acid.

3. Heat the mixture to 185°F, using a candy thermometer clipped to the inside of the saucepan to measure the temperature. Use a silicone spatula to scrape the bottom of the pan to prevent scorching. You will see curds start to form on the surface of the liquid.

4. When the liquid reaches 185°F, remove pan from heat and let rest for 10 minutes.

5. Place a fine-mesh strainer over a large mixing bowl and line the strainer with two layers of cheesecloth or a coffee filter.

MAKES 2½–3 CUPS

ACTIVE TIME = 20–25 MINUTES

INACTIVE TIME = 45 MINUTES

———————★———————

3 sprigs thyme

1 bay leaf

1 piece lemon peel (¾ inch x 2½ inches), no pith

1 gallon whole milk

2 tablespoons kosher salt

2 teaspoons citric acid (found in spice stores, vitamin stores, or online)

———————★———————

USING A SHARP VEGETABLE PEELER INSTEAD OF A KNIFE TO PEEL CITRUS ENSURES YOU GET JUST THE PEEL AND NONE OF THE PITH.

6. Using a fine-mesh skimmer, remove all the curds from the liquid and place them into the cheesecloth-lined strainer over the bowl.

7. Place the strainer and bowl in the refrigerator, letting the curds cool and drain for 45 minutes to form the ricotta.

8. Discard the liquid in the bowl and transfer the ricotta from the strainer to a covered container.

Fresh Mozzarella

You could buy fresh mozzarella at the grocery store, but who knows how long it's really been sitting there in the refrigerator case. Go online or dig out the Yellow Pages to find an Italian market or cheese shop near you. Call and ask if they have mozzarella curd. It's worth a few phone calls to track it down, because making your own fresh mozzarella is easy and will make you feel like a rock star. Don't be afraid to really pull and stretch the mozzarella when you're working with it; you want it to have elasticity.

1. In a large saucepan or stockpot with a candy thermometer clipped inside, heat the water and salt to 190°F, stirring to dissolve the salt. Set a bowl of ice water to the side. Place the mozzarella curd in a large mixing bowl.

2. When the salt water reaches 190°F, turn off the heat and ladle the hot salt water over the curd until it's fully covered. Let rest for 1 minute, then pour that water into a separate bowl, leaving just the watered curd. Do not discard the water—you will need it at the very end of this recipe.

3. Ladle more hot salt water from the saucepan over the curd and, using your hands, start to pull the curd into one ball.

MAKES 1 POUND
(FOUR 4-OUNCE BALLS)
ACTIVE TIME = 25–30 MINUTES
INACTIVE TIME = 1 HOUR

———————★———————

2 quarts water

¼ cup kosher salt

1 pound mozzarella curd, crumbled

———————★———————

SEE PHOTOGRAPHS ON FOLLOWING PAGE

4. When it has been formed into a ball, pull, stretch, and fold the curd around onto itself 4–5 times until all the lumps and air have disappeared and it has a shiny and smooth texture.

5. Quarter the curd evenly and place the pieces in the mixing bowl of salt water reserved from Step 2.

6. One at a time, form each of those four pieces into a round ball—by pulling, stretching, and folding, just like you did in Step 4—and place them in the ice water. If the ball begins to break, put it back in the salt water for a few seconds to make it pliable.

7. Fill a container with equal parts reserved salt water and ice water from Step 6 and store the mozzarella balls inside. Refrigerate for at least 1 hour before you are ready to use.

———★———

MOZZARELLA CAN BE STORED IN THE REFRIGERATOR FOR UP TO 3 DAYS.

———★———

Homemade Burrata

MAKES 1 POUND
(EIGHT 2-OUNCE BALLS)
ACTIVE TIME = 35–40 MINUTES

———————★———————

2 quarts water

¼ cup plus ¼ teaspoon kosher salt

½ cup mascarpone, room temperature

½ cup ricotta

1 pound mozzarella curd, crumbled

Burrata is fresh mozzarella's sexy cousin. It's a little silkier, a little smoother, and there's a creamy, rich filling that oozes out when you slice into it with the edge of your fork. You'll need fresh ricotta for this, so you can follow the Homemade Ricotta recipe on page 43, or pick up some fresh ricotta at the farmers' market. Burrata is best served at room temperature.

1. Heat the water and ¼ cup salt to 190°F in a large saucepan or stockpot outfitted with a clip-on candy thermometer, stirring to dissolve the salt. Have ready three mixing bowls. Set a fourth bowl, filled with ice water, to the side.

2. In a mixing bowl, stir together the mascarpone, ricotta, and remaining ¼ teaspoon salt and set aside at room temperature.

3. Place the mozzarella curd in a separate large mixing bowl.

4. When the salt water reaches 190°F, turn off the heat and ladle salt water over the curd until fully covered. Let rest for 1 minute, then pour that water into a separate bowl, leaving just the watered curd. Do not discard the water.

5. Ladle more hot salt water from the saucepan over the curd, covering it. Using your hands, start to pull the curd into one ball.

6. When it has been pulled into one ball, pull, stretch, and fold the curd around onto itself 4–5 times until all the lumps and air have disappeared and it has a shiny and smooth texture.

7. Cut this ball into eight even pieces and place these back in the salt water from Step 4.

8. One at a time, form each piece into a flat disk. With a 1-ounce scoop (approximately 2 tablespoons), place the ricotta-mascarpone mixture in the center. Form the mozzarella around it into a ball, then twist and pinch off the excess to seal it.

9. Place each completed cheese ball into a bowl of ice water. If the ball begins to break, place it back in the salt water for a few seconds to make it pliable.

10. Fill a container with equal parts reserved salt water from Step 5 and regular cold water and store the cheese inside.

———— ★ ————

BURRATA WILL KEEP IN THE REFRIGERATOR FOR 3–4 DAYS.

———— ★ ————

Mozzarella Panini with Portobello and Artichoke Pesto

MAKES 4 SANDWICHES

ACTIVE TIME = 45–50 MINUTES

———— ★ ————

4 portobello mushrooms

2 tablespoons extra virgin olive oil

½ teaspoon kosher salt

8 ounces *Fresh Mozzarella*
(page 45) made 1 day in advance,
chilled

4 individual ciabatta rolls

20 large basil leaves

½ cup *Artichoke Pesto* (recipe
follows)

Portobello mushrooms are hearty and filling, and the artichoke pesto makes this sandwich a standout. You'll need a sandwich press to make these panini crispy on the outside and melted and creamy on the inside.

1. Preheat the oven to 400°F. Clean the mushrooms with a damp paper towel; remove and discard stems. Using a spoon, scrape out and discard the gills.

2. Brush both sides of mushrooms with olive oil and season with salt. Place on a baking sheet and roast for 14–16 minutes until soft in the center. Let cool to room temperature.

3. Thinly slice the mozzarella and set aside. Cut the ciabatta loaves in half horizontally, creating a top and a bottom. Each piece should be about ½ inch thick. If not, slice the inside of both halves to size.

4. On each bottom half, evenly distribute a layer of mozzarella slices and top with five basil leaves. On each top half of the ciabatta, spread a thin layer of *Artichoke Pesto* (about 1½ tablespoons).

5. Preheat a panini press on medium high. Slice the mushrooms on the bias and place on top of the basil.

6. Close all four sandwiches and press each one in the panini press for 4–5 minutes or until the cheese is slightly melted and the bread is crispy. Keep pressed sandwiches warm in a 300°F oven while you finish the remaining sandwiches.

Artichoke Pesto

1. In a dry sauté pan, toast the pine nuts over medium heat for 5 minutes, shaking the pan often to prevent burning.

2. In a food processor, combine the toasted pine nuts, artichoke hearts, Pecorino, garlic, and salt. Turn on the processor and slowly add olive oil until a chunky paste forms (about a minute).

MAKES APPROXIMATELY ¾ CUP
ACTIVE TIME = 10–12 MINUTES

———————★———————

ARTICHOKE PESTO

2 teaspoons pine nuts

2 marinated, jarred artichoke hearts, quartered into eight pieces total

3 tablespoons grated Pecorino

1 teaspoon minced garlic

¼ teaspoon kosher salt

⅓ cup extra virgin olive oil

———————★———————

PESTO CAN BE REFRIGERATED FOR UP TO 3 DAYS.

Mozzarella Pies with Bacon and Leeks

MAKES 12 PIES

ACTIVE TIME = 1 HOUR

INACTIVE TIME = 30 MINUTES

———— ★ ————

1 cup small-diced slab bacon

5 small leeks, white and light green parts only (about 4 cups)

8 ounces *Fresh Mozzarella* (page 45) made 1 day in advance, chilled

1 tablespoon extra virgin olive oil

8 sheets phyllo dough, thawed

1 stick unsalted butter, melted

A few of these little pies with a salad and a glass of wine make a great weekend lunch. They're crunchy on the outside with smoky bacon and melted mozzarella on the inside. The leeks add a softer onion taste and bring it all together into something really great. These pies can be prepared and refrigerated up to 2 days before baking. Just cover them with plastic wrap if you're not baking them right away.

1. In a sauté pan over medium heat, sauté the bacon for 8–10 minutes, stirring occasionally. The bacon should be only halfway cooked.

2. Rinse the leeks under cold running water. Slice them lengthwise and then slice each half into ⅛-inch half-moons. Rinse leeks under cold water in a colander to remove any remaining dirt. Place on paper towels and pat dry.

3. Add leeks to the bacon and stir to coat with the bacon fat. Sauté for 8–10 minutes or until the bacon is crispy and the leeks are tender.

4. Dice mozzarella into ¼-inch cubes and place in a mixing bowl. Drain and cool cooked bacon and leeks on paper towels for 10 minutes. Line a baking sheet with parchment paper and set aside.

5. Add the bacon mixture to the mozzarella, add the olive oil, and stir to coat evenly.

6. Unfold the phyllo and cover with a damp, clean dish towel or damp paper towels to prevent it from drying out and cracking. Lay 1 sheet of phyllo on a large cutting board and lightly brush it with melted butter. Top with another sheet of phyllo and lightly brush the second sheet with melted butter.

7. Cut phyllo lengthwise into 3 even strips. Spoon 2 tablespoons of the mozzarella mixture onto the bottom of each strip, 1 inch from the bottom edge.

8. Take one bottom corner and fold it diagonally over the mozzarella, creating a triangle. Press it down slightly to remove any air and distribute the mozzarella mixture evenly.

9. As if you were folding a flag (we all learned that in elementary school, right?), fold the opposite corner up over it, making another triangle. Continue doing this until you reach the top of the phyllo dough. Place each triangle on a parchment-lined baking sheet, and lightly brush each one with melted butter. Repeat until you have made 12 pies. Keep one inch of space between each pie on the baking sheet.

10. Refrigerate the pies for 30 minutes. Preheat the oven to 400°F.

11. Transfer the baking sheet of pies directly to the oven and bake for 10–12 minutes, or until the crust is golden brown.

★

SEE PHOTOGRAPHS ON FOLLOWING PAGES

Burrata with Peas, Pickled Ramps, and Mint

SERVES 4 AS A SMALL PLATE
ACTIVE TIME = 20–30 MINUTES

———— ★ ————

2 quarts water

1 teaspoon plus ¼ teaspoon kosher salt

10 mint leaves

2 teaspoons plus 1½ teaspoons extra virgin olive oil

1 cup fresh peas

4 two-ounce *Homemade Burrata* balls (page 48), room temperature

12 *Pickled Ramps* (recipe follows)

¼ teaspoon lemon zest

Freshly cracked black pepper

———— ★ ————

PICKLED RAMPS WILL KEEP IN YOUR REFRIGERATOR FOR UP TO A YEAR.

———— ★ ————

CLEAN YOUR JARS AND LIDS BY RUNNING THEM THROUGH THE HOTTEST CYCLE POSSIBLE IN YOUR DISHWASHER.

Every spring, my wife, Stacy, and I go to her parents' house in Pennsylvania to dig for ramps—wild leeks that smell like garlic but taste more like onion. Her dad and I drive shovels into the ground to loosen the ramps from the soil, and Stacy and her mom pull them out, brush off the dirt, and fill bucket after bucket. We bring them back home and pickle them at my restaurant in large batches so we can use them throughout the year. Ramps are available for just a few weeks in the springtime—check your farmers' markets. Pickled ramps and peas go great together in the early summer and they pair nicely with burrata. The mint just brightens the whole dish.

1. In a large saucepan, bring water and 1 teaspoon salt to a boil. Set a bowl of ice water to the side. Place the remaining ¼ teaspoon salt, 5 mint leaves, and 2 teaspoons olive oil in a blender.

2. Blanch the peas in the boiling water for 1 minute, then strain and shock them in the ice water until chilled.

3. Add the peas and ¼ cup of the ice water to the blender. Purée the mixture for 3 minutes, until smooth.

4. Spoon a small pool of pea purée in the center of a serving dish. Place burrata on top, drizzle with the

remaining olive oil, and garnish with ramps, lemon zest, and remaining mint leaves. Season with cracked black pepper.

Pickled Ramps

PICKLED RAMPS

MAKES ½ POUND

ACTIVE TIME = 25–30 MINUTES

PICKLED RAMPS

2 teaspoons coriander seeds

1½ cups cold water

1 cup red wine vinegar

½ cup sugar

Peel of ½ orange (no pith)

½ pound ramp stems, cleaned (see tip below)

TIP FOR CLEANING RAMPS: CUT THE RAMP WHERE THE GREEN LEAVES START TO COME OUT OF THE WHITE STEM AND SET THE GREEN LEAVES ASIDE. TRIM THE ROOTS FROM THE BASE OF THE BULB AND REMOVE THE OUTER FILM-LIKE LAYER. THE GREEN LEAVES MAKE A GREAT PESTO (SEE SALT-ROASTED PORK TENDERLOIN WITH PROSCIUTTO AND CHARRED RAMP PESTO ON PAGE 258).

1. Toast the coriander seeds in a dry sauté pan over medium heat for 5 minutes, shaking the pan often to prevent burning.

2. In a small saucepan, bring the water, vinegar, sugar, orange peel, and toasted coriander seeds to a boil over high heat.

3. Place the ramps in a large, clean glass jar.

4. Pour the liquid into the jar, leave the jar uncovered, and let the ramps rest in the liquid at room temperature for an hour. Seal the jar with a tight-fitting lid and refrigerate.

Whipped Burrata with Toast and Thyme

Burrata is pretty heavenly on its own, but when you whip it and spread it on warm toast with fresh thyme and olive oil? It's a breakfast in bed that might earn you a little extra time between the sheets, if you know what I'm sayin'.

1. Preheat the oven to 375°F.

2. Cut the ciabatta into twelve ½-inch-thick slices. Place ciabatta slices on a baking sheet and drizzle with 2 tablespoons olive oil. Toast 12–15 minutes, or until golden brown.

3. Blend the remaining 2 teaspoons olive oil, burrata, milk, lemon zest, black pepper, and salt in a food processor for 2 minutes, until thick and creamy. Refrigerate until you are ready to use.

4. Spread whipped burrata mixture onto each piece of toast. Garnish with thyme and a light drizzle of olive oil, and season with sea salt.

SERVES 4 AS A SMALL PLATE
ACTIVE TIME = 20–25 MINUTES

————— ★ —————

1 loaf ciabatta

2 tablespoons plus 2 teaspoons extra virgin olive oil

4 two-ounce *Homemade Burrata* balls (page 48)

¼ cup whole milk

½ teaspoon lemon zest

½ teaspoon ground black pepper

¼ teaspoon kosher salt

2 teaspoons thyme leaves

Extra virgin olive oil, to drizzle

¼ teaspoon sea salt (Maldon recommended)

————— ★ —————

USE A MICROPLANE TO ZEST LEMON AND OTHER CITRUS. THIS WAY, YOU'LL GET JUST THE ZEST, AND NOT THE BITTER, WHITE PITH.

Ricotta with Charred Asparagus and Harissa Vinaigrette

SERVES 4 AS A SMALL PLATE
ACTIVE TIME = 20–25 MINUTES

———— ★ ————

4 quarts water

2 tablespoons plus ½ teaspoon kosher salt

16 asparagus spears

1 tablespoon plus 2 teaspoons extra virgin olive oil

½ cup *Homemade Ricotta* (page 43)

2 tablespoons *Harissa Vinaigrette* (recipe follows)

1 tablespoon chopped chives (½-inch pieces)

¼ teaspoon sea salt (Maldon recommended)

———— ★ ————

SPICE GRINDERS ARE INEXPENSIVE AND PERFECT FOR GRINDING WHOLE SPICES INTO FINE POWDERS. IF YOU DON'T HAVE ONE, YOU CAN USE A MINI FOOD PROCESSOR. JUST MAKE SURE YOU GRIND THE SPICES AS FINELY AS POSSIBLE.

Harissa is a hot chili paste popular in the Mediterranean. I like to use it in vinaigrettes and sauces because I love the way it amplifies the flavors of the other ingredients. It's pretty hot, but you'll be surprised at how it brings out the nuttiness in asparagus and boosts the creaminess of the ricotta in this dish.

1. In a large saucepan, bring water and 2 tablespoons salt to a boil. Set a bowl of ice water to the side.

2. Cut 1 inch off the bottom of the asparagus to remove the woody end. Use a vegetable peeler to remove the skin of each spear.

3. Blanch the asparagus for 1 minute and shock in ice water until chilled. Pat dry with paper towels or a clean dish towel.

4. Heat an indoor grill pan (or an outdoor grill) to high heat.

5. Toss and fully coat the asparagus in 1 tablespoon olive oil and remaining ½ teaspoon salt. Grill the asparagus for 2 minutes on each side, leaving grill marks.

6. Place asparagus on a serving dish, top with small dollops of ricotta, and drizzle *Harissa Vinaigrette* and remaining 2 teaspoons olive oil. Garnish with chives, season with sea salt.

Harissa Vinaigrette

1. Soak the bird's eye chile in hot water for 10 minutes to rehydrate.

2. In a dry sauté pan, toast the coriander, caraway, and cumin seeds over medium heat for 5 minutes, shaking the pan often to prevent burning. Grind seeds into a fine powder in a spice grinder.

3. In a blender, combine the roasted garlic, rehydrated chile, ground seeds, Fresno chiles, red wine vinegar, tomato paste, lemon juice, and salt. Blend on medium for 30 seconds.

4. With the blender running, slowly add the olive oil and blend for another minute to emulsify the mixture into a vinaigrette.

MAKES APPROXIMATELY ½ CUP
ACTIVE TIME = 15 MINUTES

———★———

1 dried bird's eye chile

1 teaspoon coriander seed

½ teaspoon caraway seed

½ teaspoon cumin seed

1 clove *Roasted Garlic* (page 62)

2 fresh Fresno red chiles, coarsely chopped

1 tablespoon red wine vinegar

1 teaspoon tomato paste

1 teaspoon lemon juice

1 teaspoon kosher salt

⅓ cup extra virgin olive oil

———★———

THE VINAIGRETTE CAN BE
REFRIGERATED FOR UP TO 1 WEEK.

Roasted Garlic

1 head garlic

1 tablespoon extra virgin olive oil

½ teaspoon kosher salt

———————★———————

WHAT YOU DON'T USE IN THE
RECIPE CAN BE SPREAD ON TOAST,
USED IN TOMATO SAUCE, MIXED
WITH BUTTER AND PARSLEY AND
MELTED OVER A GRILLED STEAK,
TOSSED WITH FRESH PASTA, OR
USED HOWEVER YOU'D LIKE!

A number of recipes in this book call for roasted garlic, so here's a quick, easy way to roast a whole head all at once.

1. Preheat oven to 400°F.

2. Remove as many of the outer papery layers of a whole head of garlic as you can—still keeping the head together—then, using clean kitchen scissors, snip off ¼ inch to ½ inch from the top, exposing the tips of the individual cloves.

3. Drizzle garlic with olive oil and season with salt.

4. Wrap garlic in two layers of aluminum foil and place on baking sheet in oven.

5. Roast for 30 minutes, until garlic cloves become tender, turn light brown, and feel soft to the touch when you gently press them.

Egg with Sea Urchin and Potato

I once went to Spain with chefs José Andrés, Ming Tsai, Chris Cosentino, and a few other chefs. One night in Madrid, we went to a little place where the chef sent out everything on the menu. Despite the fact that we ate well for hours, all I could think about at the end of the night was this one egg dish with the sweetest sea urchin and confited potatoes. It's one of the best things I've ever eaten in my whole life. Sea urchins are popular in the Mediterranean region and used in many Italian cuisines.

Sea urchin roe is orange-pink and resembles the appearance of a tongue. It has a fresh, briny flavor, but isn't overly salty or fishy. It's slightly sweet and buttery, with a smooth custard-like texture. You can order urchin roe or whole urchins from a fishmonger or sushi restaurant. There are videos online demonstrating how to open the urchin and remove the roe, or you could ask the fishmonger or sushi chef to do it for you.

1. In a medium saucepan, combine the potatoes, onion, olive oil, canola oil, and bay leaf. The oils should just cover the potatoes. If not, add equal parts olive and canola oil until they are just covered.

SERVES 4 AS A SMALL PLATE
ACTIVE TIME = 55–60 MINUTES

———— ★ ————

1½ pounds Yukon gold potatoes, cut into ½-inch cubes

1 cup small-diced Vidalia onion

1½ cups extra virgin olive oil

1½ cups canola oil

1 bay leaf

1 tablespoon white vinegar

4 large eggs

¼ cup chopped sea urchin roe (from 4–5 urchins)

1 tablespoon finely chopped chives

¼ teaspoon kosher salt

¼ teaspoon freshly cracked black pepper

2. Cook the potato mixture over medium heat for 5 minutes. Gently stir and reduce the heat to medium-low. Cook for 12–15 minutes, until the potatoes are nearly cooked through.

3. Remove the pan from the heat and let the potatoes rest in the oil for 15–20 minutes; they will stay warm and also continue to cook until tender.

4. Fill a separate medium saucepan halfway with water and bring it to a simmer (around 185°F). Add the white vinegar.

5. Crack the first egg into a small dish or shallow bowl. This allows you to have more control as you release the egg into the water to poach.

6. Using a spoon, stir the simmering water in one direction for 5–10 seconds, then gently add the egg. The whirlpool will help the egg come together. Repeat with a second egg. Poach both eggs in the hot water for 2 minutes, until the whites are cooked and encasing the runny yolk.

7. Gently lift the eggs out of the water with a slotted spoon. Pat the bottom of the spoon with a paper towel to blot any excess water. Set aside eggs on a plate while you poach the remaining two eggs.

8. Remove the potato mixture from the oil with a slotted spoon and place in a mixing bowl. Stir in the poached eggs, sea urchin roe, chives, salt and pepper. The poached eggs will break and mix with the roe to create a creamy dressing.

9. Transfer to a serving dish and serve warm.

———— ★ ————

USE THE FRESHEST EGGS YOU CAN FIND TO MAKE THIS DISH.

———— ★ ————

Poached Egg in Olive Oil with Salami and Potato

SERVES 4 AS A SMALL PLATE

ACTIVE TIME = 45–50 MINUTES

———————★———————

3 tablespoons canola oil

½ cup small-diced yellow onion

1 large russet potato, cut into ½-inch cubes (approximately 1½ cups)

6 ounces salami, whole

3 cups thinly sliced Brussels sprouts (10–12 sprouts)

¼ teaspoon kosher salt

Extra virgin olive oil (for poaching)

Canola oil (for poaching)

4 large eggs

2 teaspoons finely chopped parsley

⅛ teaspoon sea salt (Maldon recommended)

⅛ teaspoon onion seeds (optional)

Learning to poach eggs takes some practice, but once you get the hang of it you'll want to put poached eggs on everything. The creamy egg yolk acts almost like a dressing or sauce over the salami, Brussels sprouts, and potato in this dish when you're tossing it just before serving.

1. Heat the canola oil in a large sauté pan over medium heat and sweat the onions for 4–5 minutes or until soft and translucent.

2. Increase heat to medium-high and add the potatoes, stirring to evenly coat them in oil. Let them cook for 3–4 minutes, then stir once. Cook another 9–12 minutes, allowing the potatoes to become crispy and golden on the outside and halfway cooked in the center.

3. Slice salami into ¼-inch thick slices, then cut each slice into ¼-inch x 1-inch sticks. Stir the salami into the potatoes and sauté for 5–7 minutes, until the salami is slightly crispy.

4. Stir in the sliced Brussels sprouts and salt, reduce heat to low, and sauté 5–7 minutes. This will allow the Brussels sprouts to wilt and will keep the mixture warm while you poach the eggs.

5. In a small, heavy-bottomed pot with a candy thermometer clipped to the inside, pour in equal amounts of olive oil and canola oil until there is about an inch of oil in the pot. Heat oil to 185°F.

6. Crack the first egg into a small dish or shallow bowl. This allows you to have more control as you release the egg into the oil to poach. Gently add the egg to the oil. Repeat with a second egg. Poach both eggs together for 2–3 minutes until the whites are cooked and the yolks are encased.

7. Using a slotted spoon, gently lift the eggs out of the oil and set aside on a plate. Repeat with the remaining 2 eggs, keeping the oil temperature at 185°F.

8. Spoon the potato mixture into individual serving dishes or bowls and gently top with a poached egg. Season with sea salt and onion seeds, if using. Serve immediately.

———★———

USE A MANDOLINE TO SLICE THE BRUSSELS SPROUTS AS THINLY AS YOU CAN.

———★———

Baked Ricotta with Scallion, Speck, and Saba

SERVES 4 AS A SMALL PLATE

ACTIVE TIME = 20–25 MINUTES

———————★———————

1½ ounces thinly sliced speck

4 scallions, green part only

2 cups *Homemade Ricotta* (page 43)

½ cup grated Parmigiano-Reggiano

1 tablespoon extra virgin olive oil

2 teaspoons lemon zest

½ teaspoon kosher salt

2 teaspoons saba

Saba is a thick, rich, concentrated syrup made from freshly squeezed grape juice, also known as "grape must." Sweeter than balsamic vinegar, saba is used in both sweet and savory dishes and is only slightly acidic. I like drizzling saba over salty foods, like ham or other cured meats, because the combination of salt and sweet and acid work well together. You can find saba online and in gourmet grocery stores and Italian specialty markets. Speck is a cured, smoked, earthy ham that has that great balance of being a little salty and a little sweet.

1. Preheat oven to 400°F. Slice the speck into 1 x ¼-inch strips. Slice the scallions on the bias into ¼-inch pieces.

2. In a mixing bowl, combine the speck, scallions, ricotta, Parmigiano-Reggiano, olive oil, lemon zest, and salt and stir to mix well.

3. Transfer the mixture to an 8 x 8-inch baking dish (or equivalent). You can also use smaller individual baking dishes. Bake for 15 minutes until heated through and bubbling around the edges.

4. Drizzle the saba onto the baked ricotta mixture and serve in the baking dish with a loaf of warm Italian bread.

Quiche, All In

SERVES 4–6

ACTIVE TIME = 45 MINUTES

INACTIVE TIME = 30 MINUTES

————————★————————

1 tablespoon unsalted butter

1 recipe *Quiche Dough* (recipe follows)

All-purpose flour for dusting

3 large eggs

½ cup whole milk

¼ cup grated Parmigiano-Reggiano

¼ teaspoon kosher salt

Leftovers of your choice (see suggestions, page 72)

I love my mom and she makes a mean eggplant parm (see Joanne's Eggplant Parm, page 126), but when it comes to quiche, not so much. Every Monday night when we were kids, she would come home from work, stand in front of the open refrigerator, and just pull out whatever leftovers there were and dump them into the bowl of eggs, milk, and cheese she'd prepared as her quiche base. Days-old baked ziti with scraps of lamb and cold cuts? Yes, she really made that. After I watched her drop a whole chicken leg into the egg mixture and pop it in the oven, I decided I would never eat quiche again. Monday nights became peanut butter and jelly nights for me.

Now that I'm a chef, I've learned to love quiche. Knowing how to make the crust and the egg base makes it really easy to riff on the different seasons and try a lot of different flavor combinations. This recipe will teach you how to make a basic quiche, and you're welcome to toss in whatever leftovers you have in the fridge—just please promise me you won't throw a chicken leg in there, okay? I've also got a list of ideas of how you could use some of the other recipes in this book to expand your quiche horizons.

1. Using the butter, grease a 9-inch fluted tart pan with a removable bottom. On a lightly floured surface, roll out the *Quiche Dough* into an 11-inch circle. Wrap the dough around your rolling pin to transfer it onto the tart pan.

2. Lightly press the dough into the bottom of the pan, and press around the edges to secure the dough along the sides. Roll the rolling pin over the top of the pan to cut off the excess dough. Refrigerate the dough-lined pan for 30 minutes. Preheat the oven to 375°F.

3. With a fork, prick the dough on the bottom of the pan every half-inch or so across the surface. Place a sheet of aluminum foil or parchment paper onto the dough, and place pie weights or a few handfuls of dried beans on top of the foil or parchment to prevent the crust from puffing while parbaking it. Bake for 20 minutes. Remove the foil and weights and bake for 5 more minutes.

4. Remove crust from the oven and let rest at room temperature, while you prepare the quiche filling. Leave the oven on.

5. In a bowl, whisk together the eggs, milk, Parmigiano-Reggiano, and salt.

6. Place leftovers of your choice in the crust, covering the bottom completely. Pour in the egg mixture.

7. Bake 25–30 minutes or until the quiche is golden and puffy. Let cool for 5–10 minutes at room temperature, then gently press from the bottom to remove the outside of the tart pan.

8. Gently slide the quiche from the tart pan bottom onto a serving plate, slice, and serve.

Quiche Dough

MAKES ONE 9-INCH QUICHE CRUST

ACTIVE TIME = 8–10 MINUTES

INACTIVE TIME = 1 HOUR

———— ★ ————

1 stick (4 ounces) unsalted butter, chilled and cut into ½-inch cubes

1½ cups all-purpose flour

2 tablespoons cold water

1. In a food processor fitted with a plastic dough blade, process the flour and butter for 15–20 seconds, until a coarse crumble forms.

2. Keeping the food processor on, add the water 1 tablespoon at a time. The crumbs will start to pull away from the sides of the processor and form a dough ball. This will take 30–60 seconds.

3. Remove the dough and form it into a ball. Wrap tightly in plastic wrap and place in the refrigerator for at least 1 hour.

———— ★ ————

Suggestions for Quiche Using Leftovers from This Book

Asparagus and Harissa Quiche with Ricotta (see *Ricotta with Charred Asparagus and Harissa Vinaigrette*, page 60)

Chop asparagus and add it to the parbaked shell. Mix chopped chive with the egg mixture and pour it over the asparagus. Top with dollops of ricotta and bake. Drizzle with harissa vinaigrette.

Artichoke Quiche (see *Artichokes with Lemon, Parsley, and Olive Oil Aioli*, page 80)

Add leftover artichokes to the parbaked shell and pour the egg mixture over the artichokes. Serve with olive oil aioli on the side.

Tomato and Feta Quiche (see *Squash Blossoms with Tomato, Feta, and Basil*, page 99)

Add any of the leftover tomato mixture and feta to the parbaked shell before pouring the egg mixture in.

Crispy Potato Quiche with Bacon Gravy and Ricotta Salata (see *Crunchy Crushed Potatoes with Bacon Gravy and Ricotta Salata*, page 83)

Add the crushed potatoes to the parbaked shell and pour the egg mixture into the crust. After baking, grate ricotta salata on top of the quiche. Serve with Bacon Gravy on the side.

Pork Ragu Quiche (see *Pork Ragu*, page 132)

Spoon ragu into the parbaked shell before adding the egg mixture.

Quiche with Shredded Pork (see *Pig in a Box with Sour Orange Relish*, page 250)

Shred leftover pork and add it to the parbaked shell before pouring the egg mixture in.

Sausage and Pepper Quiche (see *Sausage and Peppers*, page 263)

Spoon sausage and peppers into the parbaked shell before adding the egg mixture.

4 jersey shore style: everything fried

YOU CAN'T BE a Jersey Italian and not do a chapter on fried food. While I love the deep-fried classics from my childhood—corn dogs, funnel cakes, fried shrimp, and French fries—in this chapter, I've included recipes that are a little more grown up and not necessarily what you'd find at a carnival or on the boardwalk.

The trick to making good fried food is keeping a close eye on the oil temperature. If you have an electric fryer at home, great! If not, I've noted how you can use a heavy-bottomed pan or Dutch oven on the stovetop with a clip-on candy thermometer to track the oil's temperature. You'll just need to keep an eye on the thermometer as food goes in and out of the pan, and adjust the heat of your burner accordingly. Make sure your oil temperature stays consistent so the outside of your food doesn't burn while the inside is still cooking.

A few safety tips: When I tell you to pat something dry before adding it to the oil, please do so. Any water on your vegetables or proteins and that hot oil is going to bubble up like crazy. Keep your face away from the pot of oil, too. Battered items can crackle, spit, and splatter oil out of the pan, so you'll want to use common sense and be careful.

Like the other chapters in this book, I've included recipes that span the seasons. You won't be able to find squash blossoms year-round, but when you do, my recipe for *Squash Blossoms with Tomato, Feta, and Basil* (page 99) is a great summer treat. In the fall and winter, you might crave *Crunchy Crushed Potatoes with Bacon Gravy and Ricotta Salata* (page 83).

Any time of year is a good time for frying, in my book.

Crispy Mushrooms with Sweet-and-Sour Apricot Sauce

Some of the local pizza joints in my hometown used to make fried mozzarella sticks, fried cauliflower, and fried mushrooms. Over time, I came to like my version of fried mushrooms, because shiitakes have more flavor than regular button mushrooms. And the sweet-and-sour apricot sauce? You might want to make a double batch—it's that good.

1. Heat the canola oil in an electric deep fryer to 375°F. If you do not have an electric fryer, use a large, heavy-bottomed pot and a candy thermometer. In the meantime, remove any dirt on the mushrooms with a damp paper towel. Remove and discard stems. Set the mushrooms aside. Line a plate with paper towels and set aside.

2. Prepare the *Basic Frying Batter* and stir the ground dried mushrooms and sugar into the batter. If the batter seems a little thick, add a little soda water until the batter lightly coats the back of a spoon.

3. Dredge the mushrooms in the batter. Fry them in small batches for 2 minutes, or until light brown and crispy. Remove from the oil with a wok skimmer or slotted spoon. Drain on the paper towels and serve immediately with the *Sweet-and-Sour Apricot Sauce* on the side.

SERVES 4 AS A SMALL PLATE
ACTIVE TIME = 40–45 MINUTES

———————★———————

6 cups canola oil (quantity may vary depending on your deep fryer)

20–24 baby shiitake mushrooms

1–1¼ cups *Basic Frying Batter* (recipe follows)

1½ tablespoons finely ground dried shiitake mushrooms

1 teaspoon sugar

½ cup *Sweet-and-Sour Apricot Sauce* (recipe follows)

———————★———————

USE A SPICE GRINDER OR CLEAN COFFEE BEAN GRINDER TO GRIND THE DRIED SHIITAKES INTO A POWDER.

Basic Frying Batter

MAKES 1–1¼ CUPS

ACTIVE TIME = 2–3 MINUTES

———————★———————

½ cup all-purpose flour

½ cup cornstarch

½ cup plus 2 tablespoons soda water

2 tablespoons vodka

½ teaspoon kosher salt

I use vodka in my frying batter because alcohol evaporates at a lower temperature, so it allows the batter to crisp up nicely and hold everything together more evenly. If you don't want to use alcohol, you can substitute more soda water.

1. In a large mixing bowl, combine all ingredients and whisk together until a smooth batter forms. Don't overwork it.

Sweet-and-Sour Apricot Sauce

1. Soak the apricots in hot water for 10 minutes. Strain and chop into ¼-inch pieces.

2. In a small saucepan, combine the apricots and all remaining ingredients. Bring to a boil, then lower the heat and simmer for 10 minutes.

3. Remove the sauce from the heat and let cool for 10 minutes. Transfer the mixture to a blender or food processor and blend on high speed for 1–2 minutes, until it becomes a smooth purée.

MAKES APPROXIMATELY ½ CUP
ACTIVE TIME = 45–50 MINUTES

————★————

6 dried, pitted apricots

¾ cup orange juice

2 teaspoons sugar

1 tablespoon champagne vinegar

½ teaspoon finely diced fresh ginger

¼ teaspoon kosher salt

————★————

SAUCE CAN BE REFRIGERATED FOR UP TO 3 DAYS. BRING TO ROOM TEMPERATURE BEFORE SERVING.

Artichokes with Lemon, Parsley, and Olive Oil Aioli

SERVES 4 AS A SMALL PLATE

ACTIVE TIME = 30–35 MINUTES

————————★————————

6 cups canola oil (quantity may vary depending on your deep fryer)

3 lemons, quartered

16 baby artichokes (or 8 large artichokes)

2 teaspoons finely chopped parsley

1 teaspoon sea salt (Maldon recommended)

¼ cup *Olive Oil Aioli* (recipe follows)

1 pinch smoked paprika

In Italy, these are called carciofi alla giudia or, literally, "Jewish fried artichokes," and they're one of the most famous dishes in Roman Jewish cuisine. They are delicious on their own, but even better when served with an olive oil aioli for dipping. I like them hot and crispy, and I usually burn the roof of my mouth because I can't wait to dig into them.

1. Heat the canola oil in an electric deep fryer to 350°F. If you do not have an electric fryer, use a large, heavy-bottomed pot and a candy thermometer.

2. Set up a large bowl of ice water. Squeeze the juice of eight lemon quarters into the bowl and add those eight lemon quarters to the water.

3. To clean the baby artichokes, remove all outer leaves until you only see fully yellow leaves. Cut ½ inch off the top of the artichoke and trim a little off the bottom stem. With a paring knife, peel the outer green part of the stem until you see mostly white flesh. Cut each artichoke heart in half lengthwise, and store in the lemon water until you are ready to fry. If using large artichokes, quarter each heart and remove and discard all the fuzz.

4. Before frying, pat the artichokes dry with a clean dish towel or paper towels. Line a plate with paper towels and set aside.

5. Fry artichokes in the hot oil for 2–3 minutes, until light golden brown and crispy. Remove with a wok skimmer or slotted spoon, drain on the paper towel–lined plate, and season with sea salt. Garnish with parsley and squeeze the remaining lemon quarters over them.

6. On a serving dish, create a bed or small pool of *Olive Oil Aioli*, place the fried artichokes on top, and finish with smoked paprika.

Olive Oil Aioli

1. In a blender, combine the roasted garlic, egg yolks, lemon juice, and salt and blend on medium speed for 1 minute.

2. With blender running, slowly add both oils. Blend for 10–15 seconds to emulsify.

MAKES APPROXIMATELY ⅔ CUP

ACTIVE TIME = 5 MINUTES

OLIVE OIL AIOLI

2 cloves *Roasted Garlic* (page 62)

2 large egg yolks

1 tablespoon lemon juice

½ teaspoon kosher salt

¼ cup canola oil

¼ cup extra virgin olive oil

THE AIOLI CAN BE STORED IN THE REFRIGERATOR FOR UP TO 5 DAYS.

Crunchy Crushed Potatoes with Bacon Gravy and Ricotta Salata

SERVES 4 AS A SMALL PLATE
ACTIVE TIME = 60–70 MINUTES

———————★———————

Some people call this Italian poutine. I prefer to think of it as a refined Jersey diner classic: "disco fries," or French fries with cheese curds and brown gravy. I remember sneaking out of the house at night in junior high and high school to cause all sorts of trouble, and around 2 or 3 a.m. heading over to the diner in town to scarf down a big plate of sloppy disco fries. This is my cleaned-up version of an old favorite.

CRUNCHY CRUSHED POTATOES

1 pound pee wee potatoes (mix of red, purple, and yellow; 1 inch in diameter)

2 quarts cold water

1½ tablespoons kosher salt

6 cups canola oil (quantity may vary depending on your deep fryer)

½ teaspoon sea salt (Maldon recommended)

2 tablespoons grated ricotta salata (or crumbled goat cheese or feta)

2 teaspoons finely chopped chives

1 lemon, quartered

(INGREDIENTS CONTINUE NEXT PAGE)

1. Add the potatoes, cold water, and salt to a large saucepan or stockpot and bring to a boil. When water reaches a rolling boil, cook for 10–12 minutes longer or until the potatoes are just tender. Drain and let the potatoes cool in the colander.

2. Prepare the Bacon Gravy: In a large sauté pan, heat the olive oil over medium heat. Add the onions and sauté for 8–10 minutes, stirring occasionally, until they are slightly caramelized and golden brown. If the onions begin to burn, add a tablespoon of water to the pan to lower the temperature.

3. Add celery and garlic to the pan and sauté for 1 minute. Add the slab bacon and sauté for 5 minutes, stirring occasionally. Add thyme and bay leaf and sauté for 8–10 minutes longer, or until the bacon has rendered all its fat and is nice and crispy.

BACON GRAVY

1 tablespoon extra virgin olive oil

½ cup small-diced onion

¼ cup small-diced celery

1 tablespoon minced garlic

1 cup small-diced slab bacon (¼-inch cubes)

3 sprigs thyme

1 bay leaf

1½ tablespoons all-purpose flour

¼ teaspoon red chili flakes

1¼ cups chicken broth or stock

Kosher salt to taste

————————★————————

A CAKE TESTER IS A GREAT WAY TO CHECK THE POTATOES' DONENESS WHEN BOILING THEM. IF THE CAKE TESTER PULLS OUT FREELY, THEY'RE GOOD TO GO!

4. Whisk in the flour and chili flakes. Add the chicken broth and whisk for 2–3 minutes until the mixture thickens into gravy. Taste for seasoning and add salt if needed. Remove from heat and let rest at room temperature until ready to use.

5. Heat the canola oil in an electric deep fryer to 375°F. If you do not have an electric fryer, use a large, heavy-bottomed pot and a candy thermometer. Line a plate with paper towels and set aside.

6. Place the potatoes on a cutting board and, using the bottom of a drinking glass (or other flat surface), gently put pressure on each potato just until they "pop." Try not to smash them; you just want a few cracks in the skin. Place another cutting board on top of the popped potatoes and gently press down to ensure they're all the same thickness.

7. Fry the potatoes in 2–3 small batches for 2–3 minutes, until crispy and golden brown but still creamy inside. Drain potatoes on the paper towels and season with sea salt.

8. Just before frying the last batch of potatoes, remove the thyme and bay leaf from the gravy and discard. Reheat the gravy and whisk to pull it all back together. If the gravy seems too thick, add a little chicken broth or water.

9. Stack the potatoes in a shallow serving bowl, top with Bacon Gravy, and finish with grated ricotta salata, chives, and a squeeze of lemon.

Fish Fries with Black Mayo

Whitebait—also called smelt—are caught with special nets and found more readily in the spring and summer. Many grocery stores with fish departments carry frozen whitebait year-round, or you can ask a fishmonger at a local market to order it for you. I like deep frying whitebait because it holds up well in the hot oil, and the squid-ink mayo is deep, dark, and rich. You can find squid ink in some international grocery stores, or you can order it online.

1. Heat the canola oil in an electric deep fryer to 375°F. If you do not have an electric fryer, use a large, heavy-bottomed pot and a candy thermometer. Line a plate with paper towels.

2. Rinse the whitebait in a strainer under cold, running water and set aside. In a shallow dish, whisk together the flour, parsley, thyme, and salt.

3. In small batches, dredge each whitebait in the flour mixture, then fry for 3–4 minutes until golden brown and crispy. Remove from the oil with a wok skimmer or slotted spoon. Drain on paper towels and serve immediately with *Black Mayo* on the side.

SERVES 4 AS A SMALL PLATE
ACTIVE TIME = 15–20 MINUTES

———————★———————

6 cups canola oil (quantity may vary depending on your deep fryer)

1 pound whitebait, thawed

1 cup all-purpose flour

1 tablespoon finely chopped parsley

1 teaspoon thyme leaves

1 teaspoon kosher salt

⅔ cup *Black Mayo* (recipe follows)

Black Mayo

MAKES APPROXIMATELY ⅔ CUP

ACTIVE TIME = 10 MINUTES

———————★———————

1 large egg yolk

2 anchovy filets (canned)

1 tablespoon squid ink

1 tablespoon lemon juice

1 teaspoon Dijon mustard

½ teaspoon kosher salt

½ cup canola oil

———————★———————

BLACK MAYO CAN BE REFRIGER-
ATED FOR UP TO 3 DAYS.

1. In a blender, combine the egg yolk, anchovies, squid ink, lemon juice, mustard, and salt and blend on medium speed for 1 minute.

2. With the blender running, slowly add the canola oil. Blend for another 30–60 seconds to emulsify.

Lemon Rings with Charred Onion Mascarpone

It struck me one night when I was squeezing a lemon over my order of onion rings: what if I made the onion and lemon trade places? That's what this recipe does. The deep-fried rings are actually preserved lemon, and you dip them in a creamy onion mascarpone. I use red onion in the mascarpone because red onions have a more pronounced flavor, and you need that to be able to stand up to the acidity of the lemons.

1. Slice the lemons into ⅛-inch-thick rings.

2. In a large saucepan, combine the lemon slices, water, sugar, lemon juice, chili flakes, and bay leaves and bring to a boil, stirring to dissolve the sugar. Reduce the heat, cover, and simmer for 20 minutes. The lemon rings should become tender.

3. Strain the lemons and discard the liquid. Do not rinse. Let the lemons cool to room temperature. This should take 15–20 minutes. While the lemons are cooling, you can make the *Basic Frying Batter*.

4. Line a baking sheet with parchment paper.

5. With a paring knife, remove the pulp from inside each lemon ring so you are left with just the rind. Place the lemon rings on the parchment-lined baking sheet and refrigerate for at least 20 minutes (or up to 24 hours).

SERVES 4 AS A SMALL PLATE
ACTIVE TIME = 50–60 MINUTES
INACTIVE TIME = 1 HOUR

———————★———————

6 whole lemons

3 cups water

1 cup sugar

½ cup lemon juice

1 tablespoon red chili flakes

2 bay leaves, dried

6 cups canola oil (quantity may vary depending on your deep fryer)

1–1¼ cups *Basic Frying Batter* (page 78)

¾ cup *Charred Onion Mascarpone* (recipe follows)

6. Heat the canola oil in an electric deep fryer to 375°F. If you do not have an electric fryer, use a large, heavy-bottomed pot and a candy thermometer. Line a plate with paper towels.

7. Dredge lemon rings in batter and fry in small batches for 2–3 minutes, until light brown and crispy. Remove from the oil with a wok skimmer or slotted spoon. Drain on paper towels and serve with *Charred Onion Mascarpone* on the side.

Charred Onion Mascarpone

1. Preheat the oven to 450°F. Line a baking sheet with parchment paper.

2. In a mixing bowl, whisk together the balsamic vinegar, olive oil, and ½ teaspoon salt. Gently toss the onions in the balsamic mixture and place them on the parchment-lined baking sheet, making sure they don't overlap. Drizzle remaining balsamic mixture over them.

3. Roast onions for 20 minutes, gently tossing after 10 minutes. You will get a nice char on the onions.

4. Let onions cool to room temperature. This should take about 10 minutes. Transfer to a food processor and pulse for a few seconds or finely dice them by hand. Don't overprocess them into a pulp.

5. Stir together ½ cup charred onions, mascarpone, and remaining ½ teaspoon salt. Garnish with chives before serving.

MAKES APPROXIMATELY ¾ CUP
ACTIVE TIME = 30 MINUTES
INACTIVE TIME = 10 MINUTES

———— ★ ————

2 tablespoons balsamic vinegar

1 tablespoon extra virgin olive oil

½ teaspoon plus ½ teaspoon kosher salt

1 medium red onion, sliced into 1-inch rings

½ cup mascarpone, room temperature

2 teaspoons finely chopped chives

———— ★ ————

CHARRED ONION MASCARPONE CAN BE REFRIGERATED FOR UP TO 3 DAYS.

Risotto Balls with Broccoli Rabe and Smoked Provolone

MAKES 12–16 RISOTTO BALLS
ACTIVE TIME = 1 HOUR, 20 MINUTES
INACTIVE TIME = 1 HOUR

————— ★ —————

4 quarts water

2 tablespoons plus ½ teaspoon kosher salt

2 tablespoons sugar

3–4 stalks broccoli rabe

1 tablespoon plus 1 tablespoon unsalted butter

¼ cup small-diced white onion

1 cup carnaroli short-grain rice

¼ cup grated Parmigiano-Reggiano

2 cups vegetable broth or stock

6 cups canola oil (quantity may vary depending on your deep fryer)

1 cup panko bread crumbs, finely ground in spice grinder or mini food processor

4 ounces smoked provolone, diced into ½-inch cubes

Deep-fried risotto balls are called arancini di riso in Italian, and when they're done well they're something you can't get enough of no matter how rich and filling they are. I like packing mine with broccoli rabe and smoked provolone because it gives them a bigger flavor. When making risotto for this recipe, it's important to stir it in one direction so as to not break the grains and allow the rice to release its natural starch more evenly. That's also why I add the stock a little at a time, and not all at once. Stirring it that way to evenly release the starches also helps hold it together in a ball when deep-frying.

1. In a large saucepan, combine the water, 2 tablespoons salt, and sugar and bring to a boil. Set a bowl of ice water to the side.

2. Trim two inches from the end of the broccoli rabe stem and discard. Slice the remaining stem, leaves, and florets in half and blanch in boiling water for 1 minute, then shock in ice water until chilled. Strain and dry completely with a clean dish towel or paper towels.

3. Pulse the broccoli rabe in a food processor for 1 minute until finely chopped. Measure ½ cup and set aside. Refrigerate the rest for a snack.

4. In a large saucepan, melt 1 tablespoon of butter over medium-low heat. Add diced onions and sweat them for 3–4 minutes until soft and tender. Don't let them caramelize or turn brown. They should remain translucent white.

5. Add the carnaroli rice to the onions and stir with a wooden spoon to coat each grain of rice. Cook for 3–4 minutes.

6. In a small saucepan, bring the vegetable broth to a simmer.

7. Add simmering vegetable broth in ½-cup increments to the rice, continually stirring in one direction. When each ½-cup of broth has been absorbed, add another ½-cup and keep stirring in the same direction. Repeat this until all the broth has been used. With the last ½-cup of broth, add the ½ cup reserved broccoli rabe and stir. When all broth has been absorbed, remove from heat. The rice should be creamy but firm to the bite.

8. Stir in the Parmigiano-Reggiano, remaining tablespoon of butter, and remaining ½ teaspoon salt. Transfer risotto to a small baking dish and cool in the refrigerator for at least 1 hour.

9. Heat the canola oil in an electric deep fryer to 350°F. If you do not have an electric fryer, use a large, heavy-bottomed pot and candy thermometer.

10. Using a 1-ounce scoop, place risotto in the palm of your hand and gently roll it between both hands to form a ball. Using your finger or the handle of a wooden spoon, make a divot in the center of each ball and

place 1 cube of smoked provolone in the hole. Form the risotto around the cheese to seal it completely. Repeat with the remaining risotto.

11. Roll each risotto ball in the panko bread crumbs, tapping off any excess.

12. Fry the balls in small batches for 2–3 minutes, until golden brown and crispy. They will drop to the bottom of the fryer, so use a wok skimmer or slotted spoon to gently move them around to prevent clumping. Drain on paper towels and serve immediately.

———★———

RISOTTO CAN BE MADE AHEAD OF TIME AND REFRIGERATED FOR UP TO 3 DAYS.

———★———

Rock Shrimp with Spicy Cherry Tomato Marmalade

SERVES 4 AS A SMALL PLATE

ACTIVE TIME = 25–30 MINUTES

————— ★ —————

6 cups canola oil (quantity may vary depending on your deep fryer)

1 8 x 8-inch sheet nori (dried seaweed)

1–1¼ cups *Basic Frying Batter* (page 78)

1 pound rock shrimp

¼ teaspoon kosher salt

1 cup *Spicy Cherry Tomato Marmalade* (recipe follows)

This is my version of shrimp cocktail. It's full of flavor with a little crispiness and just a touch of heat in the marmalade. Using nori—dark green seaweed sushi "paper"—adds a nice briny flavor to the dish.

1. Heat the canola oil in an electric deep fryer to 375°F. If you do not have an electric fryer, use a large, heavy-bottomed pot and a candy thermometer. Line a plate with paper towels. While the oil is coming to temperature, prepare the *Basic Frying Batter*.

2. Tear the nori into smaller pieces and grind into a fine powder in a spice grinder. Stir it into the frying batter. Season the shrimp with salt and dredge in the batter.

3. Add each shrimp to the oil one at a time to prevent clumping. Fry in small batches for 2–3 minutes, until light brown and crispy. Drain on paper towels and serve immediately with *Spicy Cherry Tomato Marmalade* on the side.

Spicy Cherry Tomato Marmalade

1. In a medium saucepan, combine the cherry tomatoes, sugar, and lemon juice and cook over medium heat for 10 minutes, stirring occasionally.

2. Reduce heat to low and continue cooking for 30 minutes, stirring occasionally.

3. Add the pickled red cherry pepper and salt. Continue to cook for 15–20 minutes until it thickens into marmalade. Let cool for about 20–30 minutes before serving.

MAKES APPROXIMATELY 1 CUP
ACTIVE TIME = 1 HOUR
INACTIVE TIME = 30 MINUTES

———— ★ ————

1 pound cherry tomatoes, halved

¾ cup sugar

¼ cup lemon juice

1 pickled red cherry pepper, small diced

½ teaspoon kosher salt

———— ★ ————

MARMALADE CAN BE REFRIGERATED FOR UP TO 1 WEEK. BRING TO ROOM TEMPERATURE BEFORE SERVING.

Soft-Shell Crab with Polenta Crust and Corn Purée

This dish screams summer to me. Soft-shell crabs are typically available May through September here on the East Coast. Making the polenta crust is easy and hitting it with the lime zest before eating it—you could even squeeze a little fresh lime juice on top—brightens the dish and really brings out the saltiness of the crab and the creaminess of the corn purée.

SERVES 4 AS A SMALL PLATE

ACTIVE TIME = 30–40 MINUTES

INACTIVE TIME = 1 HOUR

———— ★ ————

4 live medium-size soft-shell crabs

2 cups buttermilk

6 cups canola oil (quantity may vary depending on your deep fryer)

1 cup dry polenta (fine-ground)

1 cup all-purpose flour

1 tablespoon ground coriander seed

1½ teaspoons kosher salt

1 teaspoon freshly cracked black pepper

1 teaspoon ground cayenne pepper

¾ cup *Corn Purée* (recipe follows)

1 handful of micro cilantro (or 2 teaspoons finely chopped regular cilantro)

1 teaspoon lime zest

1. Rinse the crabs under cold, running water. To clean, hold the crab from behind and use clean kitchen scissors to cut off the front (about ½ inch behind the eyes) and discard. Lift both ends of the top shell, remove the lungs, and discard.

2. Turn the crab over and you will see a flap, known as the apron. Cut this off and discard. Note: you will see a soft yellow part. This is known as the mustard. You can keep this in, or discard. Rinse the crab again under cold running water and pat dry.

3. In a bowl, soak the cleaned crabs in buttermilk. Cover and refrigerate for 1 hour.

4. Heat the canola oil in an electric deep fryer to 350°F. If you do not have an electric fryer, use a large, heavy-bottomed pot and a candy thermometer. Line a plate with paper towels.

5. In a shallow dish, combine the polenta, flour, coriander, salt, black pepper, and cayenne. Stir with a fork to incorporate all the ingredients.

6. One at a time, remove each crab from the buttermilk and let the excess drip off. Dredge each crab in the polenta mixture.

7. Fry the crabs one at a time for 3–4 minutes, until golden brown and crispy. You may need to flip the crab halfway through the cooking time to ensure it is browning evenly. Use a spatula or tongs to gently remove the crabs from the hot oil. Drain crabs on paper towels.

8. Spoon a bed of *Corn Purée* on a serving platter. Place the fried soft-shell crabs on top and garnish with cilantro and lime zest.

Corn Purée

MAKES APPROXIMATELY ¾ CUP
ACTIVE TIME = 50 MINUTES

———— ★ ————

2 tablespoons extra virgin olive oil

¼ cup small-diced white onion

1 cup fresh yellow corn kernels

1 cup chicken broth

6 saffron threads

¼ cup heavy cream

¼ teaspoon kosher salt

———— ★ ————

CORN PURÉE CAN BE MADE
AHEAD AND REFRIGERATED FOR
UP TO 2 DAYS.

1. Heat the olive oil in a large sauté pan over medium heat. Add the onions and sweat them for 3–4 minutes until soft and translucent. Add the corn and sauté 5 minutes longer, stirring occasionally.

2. Stir in the chicken broth and saffron threads and simmer over medium-high heat for 12–15 minutes, or until the liquid has reduced by half.

3. Add the cream and lower the heat to medium. Simmer for 6–8 minutes, or until the liquid has reduced by half again.

4. Remove from heat and let cool for 10 minutes. Purée the mixture in a blender for 3 minutes or until smooth.

5. Strain the corn purée through a fine-mesh strainer, using a silicone spatula or the back of a spoon to help the sauce pass through. Stir in the salt. Reheat the purée before serving.

Squash Blossoms with Tomato, Feta, and Basil

When I was a kid, my mom grew squash in our garden, and she'd stuff the blossoms with rice and bake them. In the summertime when squash and tomatoes are abundant, this dish is a natural. I include feta in these because it's a salty, briny cheese that goes so well with fresh tomatoes. The real key to this dish, though, is the vodka batter. I use vodka in my frying batter because alcohol evaporates at a lower temperature, so the blossoms crisp up immediately. The inside won't overcook and the outside won't fall apart.

1. Preheat oven to 300°F.

2. Soak the sundried tomatoes in hot water for 10–15 minutes to rehydrate and soften them. Meanwhile, bring a pot of water to a boil. Set a bowl of ice water to the side.

3. Score the plum tomatoes, using a paring knife to make a shallow "X" on each end. Blanch the tomatoes for 2 minutes and shock in the ice water until chilled to loosen the skins.

4. Use a paring knife to pull off and discard the tomato skins. Quarter each tomato, remove the seeds, and finely dice the tomatoes. Transfer them to a large mixing bowl.

SERVES 4 AS A SMALL PLATE
ACTIVE TIME = 40–45 MINUTES

———— ★ ————

8 sundried tomato halves

4 plum tomatoes

½ cup crumbled feta cheese

¼ cup thinly sliced scallions, green part only

2 tablespoons extra virgin olive oil

10 large basil leaves, rolled and thinly sliced (chiffonade)

½ teaspoon kosher salt

¼ teaspoon freshly cracked black pepper

12 squash blossoms

6 cups canola oil (quantity may vary depending on your deep fryer)

1–1¼ cups *Basic Frying Batter* (page 78)

Sea salt to taste (Maldon recommended)

5. Drain the sundried tomatoes, finely dice, and add them to the plum tomatoes. Stir in the feta cheese, scallions, olive oil, basil, salt, and pepper.

6. Gently stuff each squash blossom with 1½–2 tablespoons of the tomato mixture, leaving a ½-inch at the opening. Refrigerate the stuffed blossoms on a tray or baking sheet for at least 15 minutes (but no more than 3 hours) to allow the filling to set.

7. While the squash blossoms are in the refrigerator, make the *Basic Frying Batter* (page 78).

8. Heat the canola oil in an electric deep fryer to 375°F. If you do not have an electric fryer, use a large, heavy-bottomed pot and a candy thermometer. Line a plate with paper towels.

9. Dredge the stuffed squash blossoms in the frying batter. Fry three at a time for 3–4 minutes, until light brown and crispy. Remove from the oil with a wok skimmer or slotted spoon. You can keep finished squash blossoms warm in a 300°F oven while frying the others. Drain on paper towels, season with sea salt, and serve immediately.

5 the family secrets: homemade italian

MEATBALLS WERE THE first thing I ever learned how to cook. When I was five or six years old, my grandmother taught me how to roll the meatballs that she'd sear in a pan with oil she'd seasoned with garlic. Every single time she made them, I'd steal a few from the hot pan as they were cooking and eat them, and she'd yell, "MICHAEL!!!!" because they were still raw in the middle.

I didn't care because the meat was so fresh and the meatballs were so good, it was impossible not to eat them, especially when the whole house smelled like garlic. Sometimes I'd roll the meatballs while she cooked them, and other times she'd let me hold the wooden spatula and move them around in the pan so they'd get nice and brown while she rolled the next ones to go into the oil. It was a team effort.

It took me a long time to realize this, but my grandmother is the reason I cook today. Her encouragement and expectations in the kitchen from such a young age taught me a solid work ethic. She instilled in me a sense of pride—that feeding people isn't just something you should do . . . it's something you should *want* to do. And, most importantly, she showed me how just a few simple ingredients can turn out amazing food that makes people happy.

The recipes in this chapter are inspired by my family—my grandmother, my Aunt Connie, my mom. Unlike the rest of the book's recipes, which are meant to be served in small portions, these recipes can feed four to six people, family-style. If you have kids, I hope you'll bring them into the kitchen and let them help with some of these recipes, and encourage them to appreciate cooking. You never know how it might one day positively impact their life like it did mine.

Calzone with Ricotta, Yellow Tomato, and Pancetta

I like fresh yellow tomatoes for my calzone sauce because they're slightly lower in acid than red ones, a little sweeter, and when they're broken down in the sauce I think they taste better with the ricotta and mozzarella cheeses.

1. Place a pizza stone on the middle rack in the oven and preheat to 475°F.

2. Heat the olive oil in a medium saucepan over medium heat. Add the pancetta and sauté for 5 minutes to render the fat, stirring occasionally to prevent burning.

3. Add the onions and garlic and sweat them for 5 minutes. Add the tomatoes and rosemary and cook for 10 minutes. Lower the heat and simmer for 30 minutes.

4. Remove the rosemary sprig and stir in ½ teaspoon salt. Remove sauce from heat and set aside at room temperature.

5. In a small mixing bowl, combine the cheeses and remaining ½ teaspoon salt.

6. On a lightly flour-dusted work surface, roll out each dough ball into an 8-inch circle. Dust with flour as needed to prevent sticking. Leaving ½ inch around the edges for sealing, spoon ¼ of the cheese mixture onto one half of each circle and top with 1 tablespoon tomato sauce.

MAKES 4 CALZONES

ACTIVE TIME = 1 HOUR, 20 MINUTES

———————★———————

2 teaspoons extra virgin olive oil

¾ cup small-diced pancetta

½ cup small-diced yellow onions

2 tablespoons minced garlic

2 cups chopped fresh yellow tomatoes

1 sprig rosemary

½ teaspoon plus ½ teaspoon kosher salt

1½ cups ricotta

½ cup shredded mozzarella

¼ cup grated Parmigiano-Reggiano

All-purpose flour for dusting, as needed

4 *Pizza Dough* balls (recipe follows), room temperature

MAKES 4 DOUGH BALLS,
4½ OUNCES EACH
ACTIVE TIME = 20–25 MINUTES
INACTIVE TIME = 5 HOURS

———— ★ ————

PIZZA DOUGH

¾ cup warm water (110°F–120°F)

½ teaspoon sugar

1 teaspoon dry active yeast

2½ cups all-purpose flour, plus more for dusting

1 teaspoon salt

2 teaspoons extra virgin olive oil

———— ★ ————

DOUGH CAN BE REFRIGERATED FOR UP TO 3 DAYS.

7. Fold each calzone, creating a half-moon shape. Press the edges together to seal. Brush the tops with a small amount of the yellow tomato sauce to create a nice crust.

8. Bake the calzones on the pizza stone until golden brown; approximately 12–15 minutes. Reheat the remaining yellow tomato sauce and serve it on the side.

Pizza Dough

1. In the bowl of a stand mixer, combine warm water and sugar. Stir in the yeast and let rest for 5–6 minutes. The mixture will begin to foam as the yeast activates.

2. In a separate mixing bowl, whisk together the flour and salt.

3. Add the olive oil to the yeast mixture. Put the mixer's dough hook attachment in place and mix on the lowest speed, slowly adding the flour and salt. Increase the mixer speed one setting and mix for 5 minutes. A dough ball should start to form, pulling away from the bowl. If the ball is not forming after 2 minutes, add a little bit of water. If the dough seems too wet and is sticking to the mixing bowl, add a little bit of flour.

4. Place the dough ball in a lightly oiled large mixing bowl. Cover the dough lightly with plastic wrap, allowing room for it to double in size. Let rise in a warm place for 1 hour.

5. Uncover and punch down the dough. Divide it into four 4½-ounce balls, and wrap individually in plastic wrap. Refrigerate for at least 4 hours before use.

Suggestions for Pizza Using Leftovers from This Book

Instead of using the pizza dough recipe for a calzone, you could always make your own pizza! Just place a pizza stone in the oven before preheating it. Preheat the oven to 475°F, and once it reaches 475°F, wait another ten minutes before putting the pizza in. This ensures the pizza stone is hot all the way through, which is really important.

Roll out the dough into an 8–10-inch circle on a semolina flour-or cornmeal-dusted surface to prevent sticking. Top with whatever you like, and bake for 10–12 minutes, until the crust is nice and golden brown.

I'm a big fan of experimenting with different pizza toppings and trying what you like best. Still, here are a few combinations you might want to try, based on recipes from this book:

Pig Pizza (see *Pig in a Box with Sour Orange Relish*, page 250)

Spoon and spread *Artichoke Pesto* (page 51) onto crust, top with your favorite parts of the pig.

Brussels Sprouts Pizza (see *Brussels Sprouts with Pancetta and Maple Glaze*, page 29)

Evenly distribute mozzarella and ricotta cheese onto the crust, then top with leftover Brussels sprouts and pancetta.

Pizza Bolognese (see *Grandma Antoinette's Bolognese*, page 118)

Spoon and spread Bolognese sauce onto the crust. After taking it out of the oven, use a Microplane to grate Parmigiano-Reggiano on top while the pizza is still hot.

Octopus Pizza (see *Octopus, Like When I Was in Greece*, page 163)

Spoon and spread *The "Grand Mother" Tomato Sauce* (page 134) onto crust, top with chopped leftover octopus. After taking it out of the oven, top the hot pizza with fresh baby arugula and drizzle with extra virgin olive oil.

Meatball Pizza (see *Meatballs, Mike Isabella Style*, page 128)

Spoon and spread *The "Grand Mother" Tomato Sauce* (page 134) onto crust. Slice meatballs in half, add to crust along with some *Fresh Mozzarella* (page 45). After taking it out of the oven, season with red chili flakes.

Lamb Meatball Pizza (see *Lamb Meatballs with Spicy Tomato Sauce*, page 282)

Slice lamb meatballs in half and distribute evenly onto the crust, along with the spicy sauce. After taking it out of the oven, top with crumbled feta.

Cheese Pizza (see *homemade cheese recipes* in Chapter 3)

Spoon and spread *The "Grand Mother" Tomato Sauce* (page 134) onto crust. Top with fresh homemade mozzarella, burrata, or ricotta. After taking it out of the oven, top with fresh basil leaves.

Dessert Pizza

If you have any Nutella left over after making the *Nutella Cookie Sandwiches* (page 296) or the *Nutella Pudding with Hazelnut Crumble and Grappa Cream* (page 308), spread some of that chocolate-hazelnut goodness onto the crust, add sliced bananas, and bake.

Lasagna

I can't think of a heartier, more family-friendly dish than lasagna. I like spicy sausage in my lasagna because I want it to have a little kick. You can use store-bought noodles if you're pressed for time, but if you have a pasta machine or a roller attachment for your stand mixer, I hope you'll at least try to make your own lasagna noodles when you can. There's nothing like fresh pasta!

1. Preheat the oven to 375°F.

2. Lightly flour a baking sheet or cutting board. Separate the pasta dough into four equal pieces and flatten them with the heel of your hand. Feed each piece twice through the widest setting on a pasta machine or pasta-roller attachment on your stand mixer. Adjust to the second-widest setting and feed the dough through once. Repeat until you have reached your desired lasagna noodle thickness. Lay the pasta on a baking sheet or cutting board and dust lightly with flour while you run the rest of the dough through the pasta rollers.

3. Bring water to a boil in a stockpot and add the salt. Set a large bowl of ice water to the side. Place the fresh pasta sheets in the boiling water for 1½ minutes and shock in the ice water to stop the cooking process. If using dried lasagna noodles, follow the recommended cooking times and instructions on the box.

SERVES 4–6
ACTIVE TIME = 90 MINUTES
INACTIVE TIME = 40 MINUTES

———— ★ ————

All-purpose flour for dusting

10 ounces *Pasta Dough* (recipe follows) (or 8–10 ounces dried lasagna noodles)

4 quarts water

3 tablespoons salt

1 tablespoon canola oil

12 ounces spicy Italian sausage links, casings removed

1½ cups ricotta

1 cup shredded mozzarella

½ cup grated Parmigiano-Reggiano

2 teaspoons finely chopped parsley

1 teaspoon lemon zest

6 cups (divided) *The "Grand Mother" Tomato Sauce* (page 134), room temperature

————— ★ —————

YOU CAN MAKE THIS UP TO TWO
DAYS IN ADVANCE. JUST STOP AT
STEP 8, COVER, AND REFRIGERATE.
WHEN READY TO BAKE, LET DISH
COME TO ROOM TEMPERATURE
BEFORE BAKING, COVERED, FOR
45 MINUTES AT 375°F.

————— ★ —————

4. Heat the canola oil in a medium sauté pan over medium-high heat. Sauté the Italian sausage for 5 minutes until browned and crumbling into small pieces. Drain on paper towels.

5. In a mixing bowl, combine the cheeses, parsley, and lemon zest. Stir in ½ cup tomato sauce.

6. Remove the pasta sheets from the ice water and dry between layers of clean kitchen towels. Cut the sheets into 4 x 8-inch noodles (or to fit your baking dish).

7. Ladle ½ cup tomato sauce in the bottom of an 8 x 8-inch baking dish. Then, layer the pasta, cheese, sausage, and tomato sauce. Repeat until you have three layers. Top with remaining cheese.

8. Cover with aluminum foil and bake on a baking sheet for 30–40 minutes. Let rest for 5 minutes before serving. Serve with remaining tomato sauce on the side.

Pasta Dough

1. Fit a food processor with the plastic dough blade and add the flour. In a separate bowl, whisk the egg yolks, water, and olive oil.

2. Turn on the food processor and slowly add the liquid. After a minute, tiny dough balls will form. If the dough is too wet and not coming together, add a little flour. If the dough is too dry and not coming together, add a little water. It should form into one ball. Scrape down the sides of the food processor bowl to fully incorporate all the ingredients.

3. Remove the dough ball and dust with flour. Knead for 1 minute, wrap tightly in plastic wrap, and refrigerate for at least 1 hour or up to 2 days. Remove from refrigerator 10 minutes before using.

MAKES APPROXIMATELY 10 OUNCES OF DOUGH

ACTIVE TIME = 10 MINUTES

INACTIVE TIME = 1 HOUR

———————★———————

1¼ cups "00" flour (or all-purpose flour), plus more for dusting

3 large egg yolks

¼ cup water

1 teaspoon extra virgin olive oil

———————★———————

YOU CAN ALSO MAKE THE DOUGH BY HAND. IN A LARGE MIXING BOWL, MAKE A WELL IN THE FLOUR AND ADD THE EGG MIXTURE IN THE CENTER. USING A FORK OR YOUR THUMB AND FIRST TWO FINGERS PINCHED TOGETHER, STIR THE EGG MIXTURE IN A CIRCULAR MOTION, SLOWLY BRINGING IN THE FLOUR FROM THE SIDES OF THE BOWL. AFTER A FEW MINUTES, YOU'LL HAVE A DOUGH BALL. KNEAD FOR 5 MINUTES BEFORE REFRIGERATING.

Aunt Connie's Pepper Rings

MAKES 24 PEPPER RINGS
ACTIVE TIME = 1 HOUR
INACTIVE TIME = 1 HOUR

———— ★ ————

1½ cups plus 2½ cups all-purpose flour, plus more for dusting

2½ teaspoons freshly cracked black pepper

2 teaspoons kosher salt

2½ teaspoons dry active yeast (¼-ounce packet)

1¼ cups warm water (110°F–120°F)

½ cup extra virgin olive oil

Sea salt to taste (Maldon recommended)

On Christmas Day, everybody on my mom's side of the family went to my Aunt Connie's house. My cousins would be playing with their new toys, but all I could think about were these pepper rings. One year, Aunt Connie had to hide them from me so I didn't eat every single one and ruin my dinner. They're so simple to make, and the flavor is so good.

1. In the bowl of a stand mixer, combine 1½ cups flour, black pepper, salt, and yeast. In a separate bowl, stir together the warm water and olive oil.

2. With the mixer's dough hook attachment in place, start mixing on the lowest speed and add the water mixture to the dry ingredients until incorporated. With the mixer still running, slowly add the remaining flour. Increase the mixing speed by one setting and mix for 5 minutes. A dough ball will form.

3. Lightly oil a large mixing bowl, place the dough ball inside, and loosely cover with plastic wrap, allowing room for the dough to double in size. Cover the bowl with a clean dish towel and place bowl in a warm spot for 1 hour.

4. Preheat the oven to 350°F.

5. Uncover and punch down the dough. Divide it into eight even pieces. On a floured surface, use the palms of your hands to roll each piece into an 18-inch rope. Cut each rope into three 6-inch pieces, and create rings

with each one by looping it into a circle and pressing the ends together.

6. Bring a large saucepan or small stockpot of water to a boil. Line a baking sheet with parchment paper. Using a slotted spoon or wok simmer, dunk each ring in the water for 30 seconds and place on the baking sheet.

7. Season with sea salt and bake for 40 minutes, rotating the pan after 20 minutes. The pepper rings should be lightly golden brown, crunchy on the outside, and slightly soft in the center. Let them cool to room temperature before serving.

Escarole Soup with White Beans and Croutons

SERVES 4; YIELDS APPROXIMATELY
5 CUPS OF SOUP
ACTIVE TIME = 2 HOURS
INACTIVE TIME = 12 HOURS
(IF USING DRIED BEANS)

———— ★ ————

BEANS

3 ounces small white dried beans
(or 1 cup of canned white beans,
drained and rinsed)

¼ red onion

1 bay leaf, dried

1 teaspoon kosher salt

CROUTONS

3 cups ½-inch Italian bread cubes

3 tablespoons extra virgin olive oil

½ teaspoon kosher salt

(INGREDIENTS CONTINUE NEXT PAGE)

This is the soup my grandmother used to make for my sister and me while we were outside playing in the snow. It's hearty and warm, and takes away the winter chill. I like eating it a day or two after it's first made, because the flavors have had a chance to settle in and get bigger. You can always double or triple this recipe and freeze some for reheating on a snowy day.

1. Soak the dried beans in cold water overnight. Drain.

2. In a medium saucepan, bring 3 cups cold water and soaked dried beans to a boil and drain. Return the beans to saucepan, and add 3 cups cold water, red onion, bay leaf, and salt. Bring to a boil, lower the heat, and simmer for 90 minutes, until tender. Remove the onion and bay leaf, but keep the beans in the liquid until you are ready to add them to the soup in Step 5 below.

3. To prepare the croutons, toss the bread cubes with olive oil and salt. Toast in a large sauté pan or cast-iron skillet over medium heat for 5–7 minutes or until golden brown, stirring occasionally. Keep at room temperature until you are ready to use.

4. To prepare the soup, heat the olive oil in a stockpot or large Dutch oven over medium heat. Add the pancetta and crisp for 5 minutes, stirring occasionally. Add

the red onion and sauté for 5 minutes. Add the garlic and sauté for 3 minutes. Add the escarole and stir for 2 minutes, until wilted. Season with salt.

5. Add the chicken broth and ¼ cup Parmigiano-Reggiano and bring to a boil. Lower the heat and simmer for 8 minutes. Drain the beans (if you're using canned beans, add them now) and add them to the soup, simmering for another 2 minutes. Stir in the lemon juice and black pepper.

6. Ladle the soup into bowls and garnish with remaining Parmigiano-Reggiano and croutons.

SOUP

2 tablespoons extra virgin olive oil

½ cup finely diced pancetta

¾ cup diced red onion

1 tablespoon minced garlic

6 cups chopped escarole

½ teaspoon kosher salt

3 cups chicken broth or stock

¼ cup plus ¼ cup grated Parmigiano-Reggiano

2 teaspoons lemon juice

½ teaspoon freshly cracked black pepper

Grandma Antoinette and Mike's Favorite Gravy

SERVES 4–6 IN SMALL BOWLS

ACTIVE TIME = 30–40 MINUTES

INACTIVE TIME = 4–8 HOURS

———————★———————

½ cup extra virgin olive oil

¼ pound pancetta, cut into ½-inch cubes

1 pork shank (1–1½ pounds), bone in (pork shoulder can be substituted)

2 links spicy Italian sausage

4 *Meatballs, Mike Isabella Style*, cooked (page 128)

6 cups *The "Grand Mother" Tomato Sauce* (page 134)

1 pig's foot

The key to this gravy is the pig's foot. When my Aunt Connie had the whole family over for Christmas dinner every year, she'd use a pig's foot in her red sauce just for my Grandma and me because that's the way we liked it. At the dinner table, we'd pick up that foot that had been simmering in the sauce all day and eat the meat right off it.

Because she knew I'd get sauce all over myself, my mom always made me change out of my dress shirt before sitting down at the table. Even today, I can't eat this gravy without getting it all over me. This isn't a sauce you toss with pasta or use in lasagna. This is gravy that's meant to be eaten out of a bowl with a spoon.

1. Heat the olive oil in a stockpot over medium-high heat. Add the pancetta, sauté for 5 minutes, and remove it from the pot. Sear the pork shank for 2 minutes on each side and remove. Sear the sausage for 2 minutes on all sides and remove.

2. Lower the heat to medium and add the tomato sauce. When tomato sauce is heated through, add the seared meats, meatballs, and the pig's foot. Lower the heat to

the lowest possible setting and cover the pot. Simmer for at least 4 hours, or all day.

3. Just before serving, remove the pork shank and shred the meat, discard the bone, and return the meat to the sauce.

———— ★ ————

YOU DON'T HAVE TO REMOVE ALL THE MEAT FROM THE SHANK IN STEP 3. YOU CAN SAVE SOME TO JUST EAT RIGHT OFF THE BONE. MY FAVORITE THING AS A KID WAS SHARING THE PIG'S FOOT WITH MY GRANDMA. AFTER HAVING SIMMERED IN THE SAUCE FOR HOURS, THE MEAT FROM IT WILL BE TENDER AND JUICY. TRY NOT TO FIGHT OVER IT.

———— ★ ————

Grandma Antoinette's Bolognese

MAKES 3 CUPS

ACTIVE TIME = 1 HOUR, 40 MINUTES

——————— ★ ———————

1 pound boneless beef short ribs, cut into 1-inch cubes (ground chuck can be substituted if you do not have a meat grinder)

2 teaspoons kosher salt

½ teaspoon ground black pepper

2 tablespoons extra virgin olive oil

2 tablespoons unsalted butter

¼ cup finely diced yellow onion

¼ cup finely diced celery

¼ cup finely diced carrot

1 tablespoon minced garlic

1 tablespoon tomato paste

¾ cup white wine (Chardonnay recommended)

2 sprigs thyme

1 sprig rosemary

1 bay leaf, dried

1 cinnamon stick

1 cup canned crushed tomatoes

1 cup chicken broth or stock

This is one of those sauces that, as you're making it, you'll be tempted to go outside for a minute just so you can walk back in the house and get psyched at how good it makes your house smell while it's cooking. You can use this sauce in the Lasagna (page 109), spooned over your favorite pasta, as a pizza sauce, or with Grandma's Potato Gnocchi (page 121). I use white wine in my Bolognese, but if you prefer red, I suggest using a fruit-forward Merlot.

1. Season the short ribs or ground chuck with salt and pepper.

2. Heat the olive oil and butter in a large, heavy-bottomed pot over medium-high heat. Sear the short ribs for 2 minutes on all sides. Remove from the pot and let rest. (If using ground chuck, brown the meat, remove from the pot and set aside. You will want to discard some of the fat in the pot before the next step.)

3. Add the onion, celery, carrot, and garlic to the stockpot and sauté for 3–5 minutes, stirring often, until the garlic is golden. Stir in the tomato paste and cook for 3 minutes. Pour in the wine while scraping the bottom of the pot to loosen the brown bits left over from searing the meat. Simmer until the liquid reduces by half, about 10 minutes.

4. Using kitchen twine, tie the thyme, rosemary, bay leaf, and cinnamon stick in a bundle and add it to the stockpot. Pour in the crushed tomatoes and chicken broth and bring to a boil before lowering the heat to simmer.

5. Using a meat grinder, coarsely grind the seared short ribs. Add the ground short ribs or chuck to the sauce and simmer, uncovered, for 1 hour, stirring occasionally.

6. Serve this Bolognese with gnocchi, over pasta, or in lasagna.

YOU CAN REFRIGERATE THE BOLOGNESE FOR UP TO 3 DAYS, OR FREEZE FOR UP TO ONE MONTH.

Grandma's Potato Gnocchi

I made this version of my grandmother's gnocchi on the Ellis Island episode of Top Chef All-Stars and they were so delicate, they practically melted in the judges' mouths. The keys to making great gnocchi are to have a higher potato-to-flour ratio and not overwork the dough. You can serve the gnocchi with Grandma Antoinette's Bolognese *(page 118),* Pork Ragu *(page 132), or* The "Grand Mother" Tomato Sauce *(page 134) and finish with freshly grated Parmigiano-Reggiano.*

1. Preheat the oven to 425°F.

2. Prick the potatoes with a fork, place on a baking sheet, and bake for 1 hour. Let the potatoes cool for 10–12 minutes at room temperature before handling them.

3. Bring water to a boil in a large saucepan or stockpot. Once the water reaches a boil, add 1 teaspoon salt. In the meantime, scoop out the flesh from the potatoes and discard the skins. Press the flesh through a potato ricer into a mixing bowl.

4. Stir in 1 cup flour, the egg yolks, Parmigiano-Reggiano, and 3 tablespoons salt. Mix with your hands until the ingredients are just combined. Be careful not to overwork the dough, or the gnocchi will become tough.

5. Using the palms of your hands, roll mixture into 12-inch long ropes (¾-inch thick) and lightly dust the

SERVES 4–6

ACTIVE TIME = 25 MINUTES

INACTIVE TIME = 1 HOUR, 10 MINUTES

———————★———————

4 large Idaho russet potatoes

4 quarts water

1 teaspoon plus 3 tablespoons kosher salt

1 cup plus ½ cup all-purpose flour

2 large egg yolks, beaten

¼ cup grated Parmigiano-Reggiano

dough with remaining flour to prevent sticking. Cut the ropes into ¾-inch pieces. Press each piece lightly with the tines of a fork.

6. In three batches, drop the gnocchi in the boiling water and remove them when all are floating on the surface, approximately 1–2 minutes.

7. Remove the gnocchi from the water using a wok skimmer or perforated spoon and serve immediately.

Mom's Broiled Chicken with Potatoes and Onions

Some people roast their chicken, while others fry it. I like mine broiled—and once you prepare it this way, you're going to wonder why you ever made chicken any other way. You could buy a whole chicken and break it down yourself, or buy a chicken already cut into pieces—breast, legs, thighs, wings—and make it even easier. When my mom made chicken for my sister and me, this is how she did it. This dish reminds me of home.

1. Preheat oven broiler on high and position oven rack in the middle of the oven (8 inches away from the broiler flame is ideal).

2. Remove chicken from refrigerator and let it rest at room temperature for a few minutes while completing the next step.

3. In a small mixing bowl, stir together the olive oil, oregano, garlic, paprika, and lemon zest until it forms a paste.

4. In a separate large mixing bowl, add the chicken pieces, half of the paste, and 1½ teaspoons salt. Use your hands to rub the paste evenly onto the chicken, then season with pepper, and arrange chicken parts skin-side-up in a large roasting pan.

SERVES 4–6
ACTIVE TIME = 20–25 MINUTES
INACTIVE TIME = 25 MINUTES

———————— ★ ————————

3–3½-pound chicken cut into parts

⅓ cup extra virgin olive oil

2 tablespoons dried oregano

1 tablespoon minced garlic

1½ teaspoons smoked paprika

1 lemon, zested and then cut into wedges

1½ teaspoons plus 1½ teaspoons kosher salt

1½ teaspoons freshly cracked black pepper

2 medium-size russet potatoes, unpeeled, and cut into 12 wedges each

16 white pearl onions, peeled

1 teaspoon sea salt (prefer Maldon)

5. In the same large mixing bowl, add potato wedges, onions, and remaining paste and salt. Toss to combine and arrange around the chicken pieces in the roasting pan, being careful not to overlap ingredients.

6. Place roasting pan under the broiler, close the oven door, and broil for 25 minutes.

7. Slowly open the door (BE CAREFUL—do not put your face near the oven door as the smoke and heat can be intense). Remove roasting pan from oven and check the temperature with a meat thermometer. The chicken is done when temperature registers 160°F and the juices run clear. Let the chicken rest at room temperature for 4–5 minutes before serving.

8. Arrange chicken on a large platter and place potatoes and onions around. Squeeze lemon wedges over dish and season with sea salt. Serve family style.

Joanne's Eggplant Parm

SERVES 4–6

ACTIVE TIME = 1 HOUR, 10 MINUTES

INACTIVE TIME = 40 MINUTES

———— ★ ————

½ cup all-purpose flour

3 large eggs, beaten

2 cups panko bread crumbs

¼ cup plus 3 cups grated Parmigiano-Reggiano

2 tablespoons dried oregano

2½ teaspoons salt

2 teaspoons finely ground red chili flakes

2 medium eggplants

2 cups extra virgin olive oil

3 whole garlic cloves

6 cups *The "Grand Mother" Tomato Sauce* (page 134)

3 cups shredded mozzarella cheese

10 basil leaves, rolled and thinly sliced (chiffonade)

Growing up, when I went to other kids' houses in the neighborhood and their mom made chicken parmesan or eggplant parm, it usually involved pasta with a dribble of sauce, some chicken or fried eggplant, and a blob of melted cheese on top. My friends would say, "Oh, this is soooo good," and I'd think, "No it's not, because it isn't my mom's." Everyone who's had my mother's eggplant parm has said, "This is awesome." She makes it like a casserole, and I like it because it's so aromatic, so simple to make, and so classic. My mom and I sometimes joke about her cooking skills, but her eggplant parm is nothing to laugh at! It's really, really good.

1. Preheat the oven to 375°F. Set up a breading station using three separate shallow bowls: one for flour and the second for eggs. In the third bowl, whisk together the bread crumbs, ¼ cup Parmigiano-Reggiano, oregano, salt, and chili flakes.

2. Slice off ½ inch from the top and bottom of the eggplant and discard. Use a vegetable peeler to remove the skin. Slice the eggplant into ¾-inch-thick rounds.

3. Dredge each eggplant round in flour, then egg, then bread crumb mixture.

4. Heat the olive oil and garlic cloves in a large sauté pan over medium heat. Sauté garlic for 10–15 minutes, until golden brown. Remove and discard garlic from the oil.

5. Increase the heat to medium-high and fry the breaded eggplant slices for 3 minutes on each side, until golden brown. Cool on a cooling rack.

6. Ladle ¾ cup of tomato sauce into an 8 x 8-inch baking dish. Layer the eggplant, sauce, mozzarella, Parmigiano-Reggiano, and basil. Repeat until you have three layers of eggplant. Top with the remaining cheese. The key is to have each layer of crispy eggplant surrounded by tomato sauce.

7. Cover with foil and place the baking dish on a baking sheet. Bake for 35 minutes, removing the foil after 25 minutes. The sauce and cheese should be bubbling. Let rest at room temperature for 5 minutes before serving.

———★———

YOU CAN MAKE THIS UP TO 2 DAYS IN ADVANCE. JUST STOP AFTER STEP 6, COVER, AND REFRIGERATE. BEFORE BAKING, LET THE DISH COME TO ROOM TEMPERATURE, THEN BAKE COVERED AT 375°F FOR 45 MINUTES, REMOVE THE FOIL, AND FINISH BAKING FOR ANOTHER 10 MINUTES.

———★———

Meatballs, Mike Isabella Style

MAKES 20–25 MEATBALLS

ACTIVE TIME = 1 HOUR, 30 MINUTES

———————— ★ ————————

¼ cup plus ½ cup extra virgin olive oil

1 cup minced red onion

4 slices white bread, crust removed

½ cup whole milk

1 whole egg

½ pound ground beef (80/20 preferred)

½ pound ground pork

½ pound ground veal

¼ pound ground or finely diced mortadella (optional, but highly recommended)

⅓ cup finely chopped mint (optional)

1 tablespoon dried oregano

1 tablespoon kosher salt

(INGREDIENTS CONTINUE NEXT PAGE)

If you grew up in an Italian-American household you had meatballs, not meatloaf, for dinner a few times a month, and every family had their own secret recipe. My meatballs are a take on my grandmother's recipe that I've evolved over the years. I wanted to make the perfect meatball with the most flavor I could get into it. And I wanted to have a soft meatball—that's where the mortadella comes in. It's got just enough fat in it to make the meatballs creamy. And the mint? That's the Greek in me. It just opens it up and makes it taste clean and not heavy.

You can serve these meatballs over polenta with a poached egg. You could braise them in tomato sauce, serve them with pasta or sautéed vegetables, top a pizza with them, or just eat them on their own. They're classic and full of flavor, so have fun with them.

1. Heat ¼ cup olive oil in a large sauté pan over medium heat. Sweat the onions for 10 minutes until soft and translucent, stirring occasionally. Remove from heat and let rest at room temperature.

2. Soak the bread in milk for 1 minute. Squeeze out the milk and mince the bread.

5. In a large mixing bowl, combine the onions, bread, egg, meats, mint, oregano, salt, pepper, and lemon zest. Mix with your hands until all ingredients are incorporated. Don't overwork the meat; you don't want your meatballs to be too dense. Roll the meat into 1½-ounce balls (a little smaller than a golf ball).

2 teaspoons ground black pepper

Zest of 1 lemon

2 whole garlic cloves, peeled

6 cups *The "Grand Mother" Tomato Sauce* (page 134)

4. In a large sauté pan, sauté the garlic in ½ cup olive oil over medium heat for 12–15 minutes, until the garlic turns golden brown. Remove and discard the garlic cloves, and increase the heat to medium-high. Line a plate with paper towels.

5. Sear the meatballs in the garlic-infused oil for 2 minutes on all sides until they are golden brown all the way around. Remove them from the oil with a slotted spoon, and let them drain on paper towels.

6. Heat the tomato sauce in a large saucepan over medium heat. Submerge the seared meatballs in the sauce and simmer for 20 minutes to finish cooking them. The meatballs are ready to serve but can be kept warm in the sauce over low heat for up to 1 hour.

Pork Ragu

SERVES 6–8; MAKES 3 CUPS

ACTIVE TIME = 40 MINUTES

INACTIVE TIME = 3 HOURS

———————★———————

¾ ounce dried porcini mushrooms

1½ cups warm water

2 bone-in pork shanks, 2½–3 pounds total (pork shoulder can be substituted—see tip)

1½ tablespoons kosher salt

2 teaspoons freshly ground black pepper

3 tablespoons all-purpose flour

3 tablespoons extra virgin olive oil

½ cup chopped yellow onion

½ cup chopped celery

½ cup chopped carrots

1 garlic clove, minced

½ cup dry white wine

1½ cups chicken stock

1½ cups canned crushed tomatoes

1 sprig rosemary

Kosher salt and pepper to taste

This ragu can be served with Grandma's Potato Gnocchi (page 121) or spooned over your favorite pasta. I prefer white wine in my ragu, because it makes it a little lighter tasting, which means I can eat more of it!

1. Preheat the oven to 350°F. In a bowl, soak the dried porcini mushrooms in warm water for 30 minutes. Season the pork shanks with salt and pepper and dust with flour. Line a plate with paper towels.

2. Heat the olive oil in a heavy-bottomed, oven-safe pot or Dutch oven over medium-high heat. Sear the pork shanks 2 minutes on each side until golden brown. Drain on paper towels and let rest at room temperature.

3. Strain the mushrooms over a bowl, reserving the liquid. Coarsely chop the mushrooms and add them to the pot. Add the onion, celery, carrots, and garlic. Sauté over medium-high heat for 3–5 minutes until garlic is golden.

4. Pour in the wine and use a wooden spoon or spatula to loosen the brown bits from the bottom of the pot left over from searing the meat. Simmer 8–10 minutes, or until the wine evaporates.

5. Stir in the chicken stock, tomatoes, rosemary, and reserved mushroom liquid. Bring to a boil and add the seared pork shanks. Cover with a lid and braise in the oven for 3 hours. After 1½ hours, turn the shanks to ensure they get evenly cooked through.

6. Remove the pork shanks from the liquid and let cool at room temperature for 15 minutes. The meat should be falling off the bone.

7. Remove and discard the rosemary sprig. Pass the liquid and vegetables through a food mill on the smallest disk (or pulse in a food processor until pureed). Return the liquid to the pot.

8. Remove the pork from the bone and shred, discarding the fat. Return the shredded pork to the pureed braising liquid and simmer for 15 minutes until it becomes a rich stew.

———★———

IF USING PORK SHOULDER, BRAISE FOR 2 HOURS, TURN MEAT AND BRAISE FOR 2 MORE HOURS. BEFORE PASSING THE LIQUID THROUGH THE FOOD MILL, STRAIN THE FAT OFF THE SURFACE AND DISCARD.

———★———

The "Grand Mother" Tomato Sauce

MAKES 6 CUPS

ACTIVE TIME = 1 HOUR, 15 MINUTES

————— ★ —————

¼ cup canola oil

1½ cups thinly sliced yellow onion

½ cup thinly sliced garlic

2 bay leaves

4 cups canned crushed tomatoes

4 cups chopped fresh plum tomatoes (blanch whole to remove skins if using a food processor in Step 3)

¼ cup extra virgin olive oil

1 tablespoon kosher salt

1 tablespoon dried oregano

1 teaspoon ground black pepper

In culinary school, you learn about the five "Mother Sauces"—béchamel, velouté, espagnole, hollandaise, and tomate—from which all other sauces are derived. I've designated this tomato sauce a "Grand Mother" sauce because my Grandma Antoinette taught me how to make it, and I use it—or a version of it—in nearly all my family-style Italian dishes. Seasoning it at the end ensures the sauce is full of flavor.

1. Heat the canola oil in a large saucepan over medium-high heat. Sauté the onions for 5 minutes, stirring frequently to prevent burning. Lower the heat to medium and stir occasionally for 12–15 minutes until onions are caramelized and golden brown.

2. Stir in the garlic and sauté for 3–5 more minutes, or until garlic is light golden brown. Add the bay leaves, canned tomatoes, and fresh tomatoes and simmer for 5 minutes. Reduce the heat to low and simmer for another 50 minutes, stirring every 10 minutes.

3. Remove sauce from heat and discard the bay leaves. Pass the sauce through a food mill on the smallest disk (or pulse in a food processor until puréed, then strain through a fine-mesh strainer). Return it to the saucepan and stir in the olive oil, salt, oregano, and pepper.

Veal Cutlet with Asparagus, Basil, and Lemon

Veal piccata was a popular dish in my hometown when I was growing up, but I like my veal dishes to have a little more depth and breadth of flavor and texture. This lightly breaded and pan-fried veal is light and creamy, and the basil and lemon brighten the asparagus salad.

1. Set up a breading station using three separate shallow bowls: one for flour, the second for eggs. In the third bowl, whisk together the panko, Parmigiano-Reggiano, oregano, parsley, lemon zest, salt, and ground chili flakes.

2. Dredge the veal in the flour, then egg, then bread crumb mixture and set aside.

3. Heat the olive oil and garlic in a large sauté pan over medium heat. Sauté the garlic for 12–15 minutes, until golden brown.

4. While the garlic is sautéing, bring a medium saucepan of water to a boil. Set a bowl of ice water to the side. Add a tablespoon or two of kosher salt to the boiling water and blanch the asparagus for 2 minutes. Shock the spears in ice water until chilled. Completely dry with paper towels or clean dishtowels. Slice on the bias into bite-size pieces.

SERVES 4 AS A SMALL PLATE
ACTIVE TIME = 40 MINUTES

———————★———————

VEAL CUTLETS

½ cup all-purpose flour

3 large eggs, beaten

2 cups panko bread crumbs

½ cup grated Parmigiano-Reggiano

1 tablespoon dried oregano

1 tablespoon finely chopped fresh parsley

1 tablespoon lemon zest

1 tablespoon kosher salt

2 teaspoons finely ground red chili flakes

1¼ pounds veal scaloppini (eight 2½-ounce portions)

1 cup extra virgin olive oil

3 garlic cloves, peeled

(INGREDIENTS CONTINUE NEXT PAGE)

ASPARAGUS AND TOMATO SALAD

8 asparagus spears, with woody ends removed

3 tablespoons extra virgin olive oil

2 tablespoons lemon juice

1 teaspoon honey

½ teaspoon plus 1–2 tablespoons kosher salt

1 pinch ground white pepper

1 cup halved cherry or grape tomatoes

1 cup baby arugula, loosely packed

¼ cup torn basil leaves

1 lemon, cut into 4 wedges

5. In a small mixing bowl, whisk the olive oil, lemon juice, honey, salt, and white pepper. Toss with the asparagus and tomatoes, until nicely coated.

6. Remove the garlic cloves from the oil and discard. Increase the heat to medium-high and pan-fry the veal in the garlic oil for 1½ minutes on each side until golden brown. Remove from the oil and place on a cooling rack.

7. Toss the arugula and basil into the salad.

8. Transfer the veal to a serving dish and top with salad. Serve with lemon wedges on the side.

6 tentacles: my greek side

THOUGH MY HERITAGE is Italian, my mom prepared a lot of Mediterranean and Greek food when my sister and I were growing up. And professionally I've cooked a lot of Greek food, so I feel a special kinship with Greek cuisine. I couldn't write a cookbook without paying a little homage to what I call "my Greek side."

I worked in Atlanta for a few years and during that time had the great fortune of visiting my chef's family in Greece, where I learned the secrets of cooking the classics. In Greece, you're not considered a chef until you can cook octopus perfectly. So, I learned how to do it and I've had octopus on the menu of all my restaurants since then.

Some people think they don't like octopus and squid because they've found it rubbery. The key to making really tender octopus or squid at home is in how you braise it. Covering the octopus keeps the steam in and lets the octopus release its own liquid into the braising liquid, which then steams it in its own juices. The vinegar in the braise tenderizes it, and the octopus liquid just intensifies the flavor. You can use a cake tester to check for doneness—it should just slide right out with no tension.

As a kid, I usually cooked with my grandmother. But the best memory I have of cooking with my mom is when we brought fresh calamari home from Chinatown after eating dim sum one Sunday morning. We cleaned it up and made *calamari classico* that night, and the combination of the tender calamari with the marinara and lemon over spaghetti was one of the best dinners she ever made. I've included a few calamari dishes in this chapter as a thank you to her for introducing me to it—and I hope these recipes for octopus, squid, and cuttlefish will entice you to prepare it at home as well.

Calamari Classico

This recipe is easy, familiar, and something the whole family can enjoy.

1. Heat the canola oil in an electric deep fryer to 375°F. If you do not have an electric fryer, use a heavy-bottomed pot with a candy thermometer to measure the oil's temperature.

2. In a large mixing bowl whisk together the flour, salt, and pepper.

3. Once the oil is to temperature, dredge the calamari in the flour mixture and tap off any excess. Fry in small batches for 1–2 minutes, or until golden brown and crispy. Using a wok skimmer or slotted spoon, gently move calamari around in the oil to prevent clumping.

4. Drain on a paper towel and transfer to a serving bowl. Repeat with remaining calamari. Serve immediately with *The "Grand Mother" Tomato Sauce* on the side for dipping.

SERVES 4 AS A SMALL PLATE
ACTIVE TIME = 30–35 MINUTES

———— ★ ————

6 cups canola oil (quantity may vary depending on your deep fryer)

2 cups all-purpose flour

1 tablespoon kosher salt

1 teaspoon ground white pepper

1-pound calamari, cleaned and cut into ½-inch rings

1 cup *The "Grand Mother" Tomato Sauce* (page 134)

Baby Cuttlefish with Salt-Crusted Potatoes and Pancetta Pesto

SERVES 4 AS A SMALL PLATE

ACTIVE TIME = 40–45 MINUTES

———————★———————

1 pound baby or petite Yukon gold potatoes

1 tablespoon kosher salt

16 baby cuttlefish

1 tablespoon extra virgin olive oil

¾ cup *Pancetta Pesto* (recipe follows)

3 roasted piquillo peppers (from a jar), thinly sliced

¼ cup parsley leaves, torn

Cuttlefish aren't fish. In fact, they're in the squid family and are often prepared similarly. Baby cuttlefish are especially tender, so they don't need the full-on tenderizing acid treatment that octopus and squid do. The pancetta pesto is a great bridge between the cuttlefish and the potatoes and pulls this dish together nicely. You should be able to find cuttlefish at an international grocery store or a fish market.

1. Put the potatoes in large stockpot in a single layer. Cover with water and add the salt. Bring to a boil and continue to boil until the water has evaporated, about 30 minutes. Shake the pot occasionally to agitate the salt. As the potatoes dry, a salt crust will form. Remove from heat and set aside.

2. Using a sharp knife or kitchen shears, cut the tentacles from the cuttlefish bodies. Cut off and discard the hard piece of cartilage. Trim any long tentacles and discard. Rinse the remaining tentacles and cuttlefish bodies under cold, running water and pat dry with paper towels or a clean dishtowel.

3. Heat the olive oil in a large sauté pan over medium-high heat and add the cuttlefish bodies and tentacles.

MAKES APPROXIMATELY 1 CUP

ACTIVE TIME = 40–45 MINUTES

———————— ★ ————————

PANCETTA PESTO

1 tablespoon plus ⅓ cup extra virgin olive oil

1½ cups small-diced pancetta (6 ounces)

½ cup small-diced shallot

1 tablespoon minced garlic

¼ cup pine nuts

1 cup parsley leaves, loosely packed

¼ cup grated Parmigiano-Reggiano

———————— ★ ————————

PESTO CAN BE REFRIGERATED FOR UP TO 3 DAYS. THIS PESTO IS MEANT TO BE A LITTLE "BROKEN" IN THAT THE OLIVE OIL WILL SEPARATE SLIGHTLY. YOU WILL NEED TO STIR TO BRING IT TOGETHER BEFORE USING.

Sauté for 3–4 minutes, then add ¼ cup *Pancetta Pesto* and the piquillo peppers. Toss to combine and heat for 1 more minute.

4. Spoon the remaining ½ cup *Pancetta Pesto* on a serving dish. Top with the potatoes and then the cuttlefish. Garnish with parsley and serve immediately.

Pancetta Pesto

1. Heat 1 tablespoon olive oil in a large sauté pan over medium heat. Add the pancetta and cook for 10–12 minutes, or until the fat has rendered and the pancetta is crispy. Add the shallot and sauté for 2 minutes. Add garlic and cook for 1 more minute.

2. Transfer the pancetta mixture to a small bowl and refrigerate until cool.

3. Toast the pine nuts in a dry sauté pan over medium heat for 5 minutes, shaking the pan often to prevent burning.

4. In a food processor, combine the toasted pine nuts, cooled pancetta mixture, parsley, and Parmigiano-Reggiano. With the processor running, slowly add ⅓ cup olive oil until a paste forms, about 30–45 seconds.

Smoky Octopus with Chickpeas and Artichokes

This dish was on the opening menu at my restaurant, Graffiato, and was a big hit. The chickpeas' earthiness with the creaminess of the octopus and the acidity of the artichokes are a natural match.

1. Preheat the oven to 325°F.

2. Combine the red wine vinegar, peppercorns, and bay leaf in a baking dish. Place the octopus in the baking dish, tentacles down and heads up. Cover with parchment paper, then tightly cover the dish with aluminum foil. Braise for 1 hour, or until the octopus is soft and tender.

3. While the octopus is in the oven, fill a large bowl with cold water. Squeeze the lemon quarters into the water, then drop them in.

4. Clean the artichokes by removing the outer leaves until you see fully yellow leaves. Cut ½ inch from the top and trim a little off of the bottom stem. With a paring knife, remove the outer green part of the stem until you see mostly white flesh. Cut each artichoke heart in half, lengthwise, and store them in the lemon water for 5 minutes. If using large artichokes, quarter each heart and scrape out and discard the fuzz.

SERVES 4 AS A SMALL PLATE

ACTIVE TIME = 1 HOUR, 20 MINUTES

——————★——————

½ cup red wine vinegar

1 tablespoon black peppercorns

1 bay leaf

3 whole octopus (½ pound each)

1 whole lemon, quartered

8 baby artichokes (or 4 large artichokes)

3 tablespoons extra virgin olive oil

1½ tablespoons lemon juice

1 teaspoon kosher salt

1 cup *Chickpea Purée* (recipe follows)

1 tablespoon finely chopped chives

5. Remove the artichokes from the lemon water and thinly slice. Transfer to a bowl and toss with olive oil, lemon juice, and salt. Marinate at room temperature until you are ready to use.

6. When the octopus is finished braising, remove them from the baking dish and let them rest at room temperature until cool enough to handle. Remove the tentacles from the bodies and discard the bodies.

7. Heat an indoor grill pan or an outdoor grill to medium-high heat. Strain the artichokes from the marinade and reserve the marinade. Lightly brush the octopus tentacles with the reserved marinade and grill for 1–2 minutes on each side or until nicely charred with grill marks. The octopus is already fully cooked, so you are just adding a smoky flavor.

8. Spoon some *Chickpea Purée* onto a serving dish and top with octopus. Garnish with marinated artichokes and chives.

Chickpea Purée

1. In a medium saucepan, cover the chickpeas with water, bring to a boil, then drain.

2. Toast coriander seeds in a dry sauté pan over medium heat for 5 minutes, shaking the pan often to prevent burning. Grind seeds into a fine powder in a spice grinder or mini food processor.

3. Put the chickpeas, coriander powder, olive oil, lemon juice, and salt into a food processor and process, slowly adding the water while the food processor is running. Process for 5 minutes until the mixture is smooth, stopping only to scrape down the sides of the processor bowl.

MAKES APPROXIMATELY 1 CUP
ACTIVE TIME = 20–25 MINUTES

———————★———————

1 (15-ounce) can chickpeas, drained and rinsed

2 teaspoons coriander seeds

2 tablespoons extra virgin olive oil

2 tablespoons lemon juice

1 teaspoon kosher salt

2 tablespoons water

———————★———————

CHICKPEA PURÉE CAN BE REFRIGERATED FOR UP TO 5 DAYS.

Calamari Crostini with Balsamic and Arugula

MAKES 16 PIECES

ACTIVE TIME = 1 HOUR, 10 MINUTES

———————— ★ ————————

4 slices white bread

1 cup balsamic vinegar

1 tablespoon sugar

2 cloves *Roasted Garlic* (see page 62)

½ pound calamari, cleaned, bodies only

8 mint leaves

3 scallions, thinly sliced, green part only

Zest of ½ lemon

1 whole large egg, beaten

1 tablespoon extra virgin olive oil

2 teaspoons cornstarch

½ teaspoon kosher salt

6 cups canola oil (quantity may vary depending on your deep fryer)

½ cup arugula

You might consider making these crostini as an accompaniment to the Warm Octopus Salad with Potato, Kalamata Olives, and Pancetta (page 161). They're crunchy and salty, and the balsamic vinegar and arugula round out each bite.

1. Preheat the oven to 250°F.

2. Remove the crust from the bread. Cut each slice twice diagonally, creating 4 triangles per slice. Arrange the bread in a single layer on a baking sheet, and toast in the oven for 30 minutes. Remove and set aside, but keep the oven on.

3. In a small saucepan, bring the balsamic vinegar and sugar to a boil. Lower the heat to medium-low, reduce the liquid to ¼ cup, and set aside at room temperature. Reducing the liquid should take 15–20 minutes, but keep an eye on it to see when it gets thick and syrupy— you don't want it to burn!

4. In a food processor, combine the roasted garlic, calamari, mint, scallions, lemon zest, egg, olive oil, cornstarch, and salt. Process for 2–3 minutes, or until a paste forms.

5. Heat the canola oil in an electric deep fryer to 350°F. If you do not have a deep fryer, use a heavy-bottomed pot and candy thermometer. Line a plate with paper towels.

6. Evenly spread 1 tablespoon of the calamari mixture onto each piece of bread. In batches of 2 or 3, add bread slices to the oil, calamari side down. The bread should float to the top and begin bubbling. Fry for about a minute, then use a slotted spoon or wok skimmer to carefully flip the bread, and fry for 15 seconds longer.

7. Remove the bread from the oil and drain on paper towels. Place finished crostini on a baking sheet in the warm oven to keep them hot. Arrange the crostini on a serving dish, top with arugula, and drizzle with the balsamic reduction.

Squid with Melted Cherry Tomatoes and Ink Bread Crumbs

SERVES 4 AS A SMALL PLATE

ACTIVE TIME = 1 HOUR, 10 MINUTES

——————— ★ ———————

Cooking with squid ink shouldn't be intimidating. It's easy to find in the international section of your grocery store or in an Asian market. You can also order it online.

1. Bring a large pot of water to a boil. Set a bowl of ice water to the side.

2. Use a paring knife to score the cherry tomatoes by slicing a shallow "X" on the stem end. Blanch for 30–45 seconds. Shock the tomatoes in the ice water, then peel and discard the skins.

3. Heat the olive oil in a large saucepan over medium heat. Add the shallots and sweat them for 3–4 minutes, then add garlic and sweat 2 minutes longer. Add the canned crushed tomatoes, Thai basil, and red chili flakes and simmer for 5–6 minutes, stirring occasionally. Add the peeled cherry tomatoes and cook for another 6–7 minutes.

4. Remove the Thai basil sprigs and stir in ½ teaspoon salt and black pepper. Remove from heat and let rest at room temperature.

5. Prepare the Ink Bread Crumbs: in a small mixing bowl, whisk together the squid ink and olive oil. Toss with the panko, and sauté the mixture in a medium

2 cups cherry tomatoes

¼ cup extra virgin olive oil

¼ cup small-diced shallots

2 tablespoons thinly sliced garlic

1 cup canned crushed tomatoes

12 sprigs Thai basil (can use regular basil)

¼ teaspoon red chili flakes

½ teaspoon plus 1 teaspoon kosher salt

¼ teaspoon freshly cracked black pepper

1 pound whole calamari tubes, cleaned

1 tablespoon canola oil

10 fresh Thai basil leaves, rolled and thinly sliced (chiffonade) (can use regular basil)

Drizzle of extra virgin olive oil

(INGREDIENTS CONTINUE NEXT PAGE)

INK BREAD CRUMBS

2 tablespoons extra virgin olive oil

2 teaspoons squid ink

½ cup panko bread crumbs

1 tablespoon finely chopped parsley

sauté pan over medium heat for 12–14 minutes. Remove from heat and let cool slightly. Toss in the parsley.

6. Butterfly the clean calamari tubes and lay them flat on a cutting board. Cut into ½-inch strips on the bias, then rotate your knife 45 degrees and slice across the strips to create diamond-shape pieces. Season squid with remaining salt.

7. Heat the canola oil in a large sauté pan over high heat and sauté the calamari for 45–60 seconds. Add the tomato sauce and toss to coat the calamari. Transfer to a serving dish and garnish with squid Ink Bread Crumbs and basil. Finish with a drizzle of olive oil.

Cuttlefish "Tagliatelle" with Squash, Black Olives, and Almonds

SERVES 4 AS A SMALL PLATE

ACTIVE TIME = 40–45 MINUTES

———————★———————

1 small zucchini

1 small yellow squash

3 tablespoons slivered almonds

1 orange

¾ pound cuttlefish, cleaned, bodies only

¼ cup extra virgin olive oil

4 cloves garlic, thinly sliced

10 Kalamata olives, pitted and chopped

6 basil leaves, chiffonade

¼ teaspoon sea salt (Maldon recommended)

A chef's most important tool is a knife, and the same is true for easy, fast home cooking, too. Be sure to sharpen your knives regularly, whether you do it yourself on a whetstone or have them done at a kitchen or hardware store. A sharp chef's knife is essential to making this dish because you'll be transforming your cuttlefish into long pasta-like noodles. It doesn't require fancy gadgets or extraneous tools, just a sharp knife.

1. Cut the ends off the zucchini and yellow squash and discard. Halve and quarter them lengthwise, then slice down the center to remove the seeds. Cut the zucchini and squash into a ¼-inch dice.

2. Toast the almonds in a dry sauté pan over medium heat for 5 minutes, shaking the pan often to prevent burning.

3. Zest the orange and set aside zest. Supreme the orange (see page 39 for directions) and cut each supreme into thirds.

4. Rinse the cuttlefish under cold water and pat dry with paper towels. With a very sharp knife, cut it into thin, ribbon-like strips. Set aside.

5. Heat the oil and garlic in a large sauté pan over medium heat and sauté the garlic until fragrant and slightly golden. Add the yellow squash and zucchini and toss to coat in the garlic oil. Sauté for 4–5 minutes, or until softened. Add the cuttlefish strips and sauté 1 minute longer. Toss in the toasted almonds, olives, orange zest, orange segments, and basil.

6. Transfer everything to a serving bowl and season with the sea salt. Serve immediately.

Spicy Calamari with Saffron Yogurt

SERVES 4 AS A SMALL PLATE

ACTIVE TIME = 30 MINUTES

INACTIVE TIME = 1 HOUR

————————★————————

3 tablespoons chili garlic paste

2 tablespoons water

1 tablespoon tomato paste

1-pound squid, cleaned and cut into ½-inch rings

2 cups all-purpose flour

¼ cup cornstarch

1 tablespoon kosher salt

6 cups canola oil (quantity may vary depending on your deep fryer)

¾ cup *Saffron Yogurt* (recipe follows)

————————★————————

CHILI GARLIC PASTE CAN BE FOUND IN THE INTERNATIONAL SECTION OF YOUR GROCERY STORE.

A little saffron goes a long way, and in this dish its aromatic headiness deepens the flavor of the garlicky calamari.

1. In a large mixing bowl, whisk together the chili paste, water, and tomato paste. Stir in the calamari, getting it evenly coated with the tomato mixture, cover the bowl with plastic wrap, and marinate in the refrigerator for 1 hour or up to 12 hours.

2. In a shallow bowl, whisk together the flour, cornstarch, and salt.

3. Heat the canola oil in an electric deep fryer to 375°F. If you do not have an electric fryer, use a heavy-bottomed pot and a candy thermometer. Line a plate with paper towels.

4. Dredge the calamari in the flour mixture and tap off any excess. Fry in small batches for 1–2 minutes, or until golden brown and crispy. Using a wok skimmer or slotted spoon, gently move calamari around in the oil to prevent clumping.

5. Drain calamari on paper towels and transfer to a serving platter. Serve immediately with *Saffron Yogurt* on the side.

Saffron Yogurt

1. Grind the saffron threads and salt into a powder using a spice grinder.

2. Transfer saffron powder to a small mixing bowl and stir in yogurt, olive oil, and lemon juice. Let rest at room temperature for 30 minutes to allow saffron to bloom.

MAKES ¾ CUP

ACTIVE TIME = 10 MINUTES

INACTIVE TIME = 30 MINUTES

————★————

½ teaspoon saffron threads

½ teaspoon kosher salt

¾ cup plain Greek yogurt (or one 7-ounce container)

1 teaspoon extra virgin olive oil

1 teaspoon lemon juice

————★————

SAFFRON YOGURT CAN BE REFRIGERATED FOR UP TO 5 DAYS.

Stuffed Baby Squid with Scallop, Shiitake, and Tomato

SERVES 4 AS A SMALL PLATE

ACTIVE TIME = 30 MINUTES

INACTIVE TIME = 30 MINUTES

———— ★ ————

3 tablespoons extra virgin olive oil

½ cup small-diced onion

¼ pound shiitake mushrooms, small-diced

1 tablespoon minced garlic

½ teaspoon kosher salt

12 whole baby squid (around 4–5 inches each), cleaned

3 scallops (U10 or U12)

¼ cup panko bread crumbs

Zest of ½ lemon

1 tablespoon chopped basil

2 cups *The "Grand Mother" Tomato Sauce* (page 134)

Italian bread, sliced and toasted (optional)

Growing up in Jersey, someone's mom was always making stuffed shells with tomato and ricotta. I love the smell of tomatoes cooking, so I decided to incorporate that into this dish and stuff baby squid instead. The texture and creaminess of the scallop, shiitake, and bread crumbs inside the squid is delicious, and the basil and lemon zest open it up and give it extra-fresh flavor.

1. Preheat the oven to 375°F.

2. Heat the olive oil in a large sauté pan over medium heat. Add the onions and sweat them for 2–3 minutes, until soft and translucent. Add the shiitakes and cook for 3 minutes longer, until soft. Add garlic and salt, cook for 1 minute longer, then transfer to a large mixing bowl to cool.

3. Rinse the squid under cold, running water and remove the tentacles with a sharp knife. Set the bodies aside for stuffing.

4. Pulse the tentacles and scallops in a food processor about 10–12 times to chop them into small pieces. Stir them into the mushroom mixture along with the bread crumbs, lemon zest, and basil.

5. Transfer the mixture to a pastry bag or a large Ziploc bag with ½ inch of the corner snipped off. Pipe the filling evenly into each calamari tube, stopping about ½ inch from the opening. Don't overstuff them.

6. Place stuffed squid in an 8 x 8-inch baking dish and cover with tomato sauce. Cover the dish with aluminum foil and place on a baking sheet in the oven. Bake for 30–35 minutes. Serve immediately, with toasted Italian bread on the side to mop up any leftover sauce on your plate.

Warm Octopus Salad with Potato, Kalamata Olives, and Pancetta

This is a Mediterranean classic. So simple to make, and packed full of big flavors.

1. Preheat oven to 325°F.

2. Combine the red wine vinegar, peppercorns, and bay leaf in a baking dish. Place the octopus in the baking dish, tentacles down and heads up. Place a piece of parchment paper on top and cover the baking dish tightly with aluminum foil. Braise for 1 hour, or until the octopus is soft and tender and has released a lot of its natural juices. You can use a cake tester to determine doneness: if it slides out with no tension, the octopus is done.

3. While the octopus is in the oven, make the *Egg Pesto*.

4. Place the potatoes in a medium saucepan and cover with cold water. Bring to a boil over high heat and boil for 10–12 minutes, or until the potatoes are fork tender. Drain, and when potatoes are cool enough to handle, slice into ½-inch-thick discs.

5. When the octopus has finished braising, remove it from the liquid. When it is cool enough to handle, cut the tentacles from the bodies and discard the bodies. Slice each tentacle into 1-inch pieces.

6. Heat the olive oil in a large sauté pan over medium heat. Add the pancetta and sauté for 6–7 minutes, until

SERVES 4 AS A SMALL PLATE

ACTIVE TIME = 1 HOUR, 30 MINUTES

——————————★——————————

½ cup red wine vinegar

1 tablespoon black peppercorns

1 bay leaf

3 whole octopus (around ½ pound each)

1 cup *Egg Pesto* (recipe follows)

½ pound fingerling potatoes

½ teaspoon extra virgin olive oil

½ cup small-diced pancetta

8 Kalamata olives, pitted and quartered

1 tablespoon lemon juice

(INGREDIENTS CONTINUE NEXT PAGE)

EGG PESTO

3 large eggs

3 tablespoons chopped walnuts

1 tablespoon chopped capers

1 tablespoon chopped dill

¼ teaspoon kosher salt

¼ cup extra virgin olive oil

crispy. Remove the pancetta with a slotted spoon and drain on paper towels.

7. Add the octopus to the sauté pan, toss to coat in the rendered pancetta fat, and sauté for 1–2 minutes. Stir in the potatoes and cooked pancetta and sauté for 1 minute longer.

8. Transfer the octopus mixture to a large mixing bowl and, while still hot, toss in olives, *Egg Pesto*, and lemon juice. Transfer to a serving bowl or individual salad plates. Serve immediately.

Egg Pesto

1. Place the eggs in a medium saucepan and cover with cold water. Bring water to a boil and cover the pan. Remove from heat and let rest for 12 minutes.

2. Toast the walnuts in a dry sauté pan over medium heat for 5 minutes, shaking the pan often to prevent burning.

3. Drain the eggs and run them under cold water to chill them more quickly. Peel the eggs and finely chop the yolks and whites together.

4. In a mixing bowl, stir together the eggs, toasted walnuts, capers, dill, and salt. Drizzle in the olive oil and stir to incorporate.

Octopus, Like When I Was in Greece

In Greece, they say you're not a chef until you can cook octopus perfectly. I like octopus braised or grilled— and no matter how you cook it, the key to bringing out the most flavor is to hit it with acid just before serving—in this case, fresh lemon juice. It opens up the palate so you can really taste the octopus. It is very important to buy the freshest octopus you can for this recipe.

1. Preheat an outdoor grill or an indoor grill pan to medium-high heat.

2. Using a knife or kitchen shears, remove octopus tentacles from the body, discarding the body. Place the tentacles between two pieces of plastic wrap. Using a flat mallet, gently pound them just enough to tenderize the meat.

3. In a large mixing bowl, toss the tentacles with canola oil and salt.

4. Grill the tentacles for 4–5 minutes on each side, then let rest on a cutting board for 2 minutes.

5. Slice the tentacles on the bias into ½-inch pieces. Drizzle with olive oil, lemon juice, and oregano. Serve immediately.

SERVES 4 AS A SMALL PLATE

ACTIVE TIME = 30–35 MINUTES

———————★———————

1 large fresh octopus (5 pounds)

1 tablespoon canola oil

2 teaspoons kosher salt

2 tablespoons extra virgin olive oil

2 tablespoons fresh lemon juice

1 teaspoon dried oregano

7 not your sunday macaroni

SUNDAY DINNER IN Italian families is all about macaroni—the word we use for almost any kind of pasta. Over the course of my career, I've found that I really enjoy making fresh pasta and experimenting with different flavor profiles in my pasta dough. In my Italian-inspired restaurant, Graffiato, I always have four or five different pastas on the menu that incorporate what's fresh and available during the season. This chapter showcases lots of fun flavors of pasta you can make at home, and the accompanying sauces and extras that go with it.

You'll see that I don't include salt in any of the recipes for my pasta doughs. I think it's more important to salt the pasta water correctly—one tablespoon kosher salt per every quart of water. Your pasta water should taste like the ocean—that's how you get the best flavor out of your pasta.

If you have a stand mixer, you'll need the pasta rollers and cutter attachments to make some of these pastas. Or, you can buy a standalone pasta machine, if you wish. If not, you can always use well-made artisanal fresh pasta from your farmers' market or grocery store in many of these recipes.

If you're willing to learn, making fresh pasta is really pretty easy and takes almost no time at all. You probably already have all the ingredients you need: flour, eggs, water, and oil. In terms of tools, you need your hands or a food processor. From there, the possibilities are endless.

Black Spaghetti with Clams, Pancetta, and Red Chili

SERVES 4 AS A SMALL PLATE

ACTIVE TIME = 55–60 MINUTES

——————★——————

10 ounces *Squid Ink Pasta Dough* **(recipe follows)**

1 cup chicken broth

1 cup white wine

2 pounds littleneck clams, rinsed under cold, running water

1 tablespoon extra virgin olive oil

½ cup small-diced pancetta

2 tablespoons minced shallot

1 tablespoon minced garlic

¼ teaspoon red chili flakes

1 tablespoon unsalted butter

1 tablespoon fresh lemon juice

1 tablespoon finely chopped parsley

1 tablespoon finely chopped basil

You'll need squid ink for this pasta, which you can find at a local Asian supermarket or from a fishmonger. In Italy, this dish is called spaghetti al nero de seppia. I just call it good. The squid ink pasta has an inherent seafood taste to it, and the heat of the chili flakes brings it all together with the clams. The parsley and basil make it fresh and bright.

1. Cut the *Squid Ink Pasta Dough* into 1-inch cubes. Using a pasta extruder fitted with the spaghetti attachment, place the pieces one at a time into the powered extruder. Spaghetti will begin to form and cut at around 8 inches long. Toss with a little flour to prevent sticking and clumping, and place spaghetti on a parchment-lined baking sheet and refrigerate. (If you do not have a pasta extruder you can use a pasta machine to create pasta sheets, then cut them with a spaghetti cutter.)

2. Bring a large pot of salted water to a boil. A good rule of thumb is to use 1 tablespoon of kosher salt per quart of water in your pot.

3. In a separate large saucepan or stockpot, bring the chicken broth and wine to a boil over medium-high heat. Add the clams, cover with a lid, and simmer for 4½–5 minutes, or until all the clams have opened. Remove the clams with a slotted spoon and continue to

boil the liquid until it reduces by half. Remove clams from their shells and discard the shells. Discard any clams that didn't open.

4. In a large sauté pan over high heat, sauté the pancetta in olive oil for 3 minutes or until just crispy. Add shallot, garlic, and chili flakes and sauté for 3 minutes.

5. Once the pot of water comes to a boil, take the spaghetti out of the refrigerator. Gently drop the spaghetti into the boiling water and cook for 1–1½ minutes, until al dente.

6. Reserve ¼ cup of the cooking water before draining the spaghetti. Drain the spaghetti.

7. Add the reserved pasta water and spaghetti to the sauté pan. Add the clams, reduced clam broth, and butter. Toss to coat the spaghetti, and when the butter is melted, toss in the lemon juice, parsley, and basil.

8. Transfer the pasta to a large serving bowl or individual bowls for serving.

Squid Ink Pasta Dough

MAKES APPROXIMATELY 10
OUNCES OF DOUGH

ACTIVE TIME = 5 MINUTES

INACTIVE TIME = 1 HOUR

——————★——————

1¼ cups "00" flour (or all-purpose
flour), plus more for dusting

3 large egg yolks

2½ tablespoons water

1 tablespoon extra virgin olive oil

1 tablespoon squid ink

1. Add the flour to a food processor fitted with a plastic dough blade.

2. In a separate bowl, whisk the egg yolks, water, olive oil, and squid ink. Turn on the food processor and slowly add the liquid. After a minute, tiny dough balls will form. Stop and scrape down the inside of the food processor bowl to fully incorporate all the ingredients. If the dough is too wet and not coming together, add a little flour. If the dough is too dry and not coming together, add a little water. It should form into one ball.

3. Remove the dough ball and dust with flour. Knead for 1 minute, wrap tightly in plastic wrap, and refrigerate for at least 1 hour or up to 2 days. Remove from refrigerator 10 minutes before using.

Corn Agnolotti with Pine Nuts and Chanterelles

This dish was on the menu for the first four months my restaurant, Graffiato, was open. It was by far the most popular pasta dish all summer, and people were really sad when corn went out of season and we had to take it off the menu. This is one of my most favorite dishes we've ever done.

1. Using a sharp chef's knife, slice the corn kernels off the cobs and use the back of your knife to extract extra corn juice. You should have 4 cups of kernels with juice.

2. In a food processor, blend the corn kernels and juice for 1½ minutes for a smooth purée.

3. Place a fine-mesh strainer over a mixing bowl and pour the corn purée through the strainer, pressing on the solids with the back of a spoon to push through as much liquid as possible. This should yield 1½ cups corn juice. Discard the solids in the strainer.

4. In a small saucepan, bring the corn juice to a simmer over medium-high heat, whisking as the juice begins to simmer. Lower the heat to medium and continue to whisk for 2 minutes longer to allow the corn juice to thicken. Remove from heat and whisk in the mascarpone and ¼ teaspoon salt to create a pudding-like texture. If it's too thin, whisk in a paste of 1 tablespoon water plus 2 teaspoons cornstarch while liquid is simmering.

SERVES 4 AS A SMALL PLATE
ACTIVE TIME = 1 HOUR, 30 MINUTES

———— ★ ————

10 ears of fresh sweet corn

⅓ cup mascarpone

¼ teaspoon plus ½ teaspoon kosher salt

2 teaspoons cornstarch (optional; see Step 4 below)

10 ounces *Pasta Dough* (page 111)

Semolina flour for dusting

All-purpose flour for dusting

3 tablespoons pine nuts

1 tablespoon canola oil

3 cups cleaned chanterelle mushrooms

5 tablespoons unsalted butter, cubed

2 tablespoons plus 2 tablespoons grated Parmigiano-Reggiano

1 tablespoon chopped chives

5. Transfer to a bowl, cover, and refrigerate for 30 minutes or up to 2 days. When chilled, put the corn filling into a pastry bag or Ziploc bag with ½ inch snipped off the corner just before piping.

6. Divide the pasta dough into two equal pieces. Flatten with the heel of your hand, then roll the first piece of pasta dough through a pasta machine on the widest setting twice. Fold it lengthwise, and roll it through one more time.

7. Adjust rollers to next setting and roll pasta sheet through one time. Adjust rollers to next setting and put pasta sheet through again. Continue this until you have reached the fifth-widest setting of your pasta rollers. You may need to cut the pasta sheet in half depending on the size of your work surface. Lay the rolled pasta sheet on a flat, lightly floured surface.

8. Repeat with second piece of pasta dough.

9. Dust a baking sheet (that will fit into your refrigerator) with semolina flour. Set aside.

10. With the pasta on a lightly floured flat surface, pipe the corn filling in a straight line on the pasta sheet, about ½ inch up from the bottom edge. Fold the bottom up and press it into the top of the pasta sheet, leaving ½ inch of space for the filling to move into. Press all the way down the long line of the pasta to seal it closed into a sort of tube.

11. Starting at one end, use your thumb and forefinger to pinch this long tube of pasta in 1-inch increments to create little "pillows." Doing this will compress the filling more tightly and create a pinched, sealed space

(about ¾ inch) between each pillow for you to separate them into individual agnolotti in the next step.

12. Run a serrated pasta cutter or crimped pastry wheel along the top edge of the folded-over dough to trim off the excess. Don't cut it too close to the filling, or you'll risk it leaking out or breaking apart in the boiling water.

13. Then, rolling it away from you, use the pasta cutter or pastry wheel to cut through the center of the pinched area between each pillow, creating the agnolotti. You can press down again around each edge to make sure they are sealed. Place individual agnolotti on the semolina-dusted tray in a single layer. You should have 45–50 pieces. Refrigerate for 20 minutes.

14. Bring a pot of salted water to a boil. A good rule of thumb is to use 1 tablespoon of kosher salt per quart of water in your pot.

15. Meanwhile, in a dry sauté pan, toast the pine nuts over medium heat for 5 minutes, shaking the pan often to prevent burning.

16. Heat the canola oil in a large sauté pan over medium-high heat. Sauté the chanterelles for 5–7 minutes, or until soft and tender, and season with remaining ½ teaspoon salt. Keep warm.

17. When the pot of water is at a full boil, drop in half the agnolotti and cook for 2 minutes. Meanwhile, stir butter into the warm chanterelles.

18. Remove the cooked agnolotti with a slotted spoon or wok skimmer and gently toss with the chanterelles, as the butter continues to melt.

19. Cook the remaining agnolotti and add them to the sauté pan. Then add 2 tablespoons of the Parmigiano-Reggiano and gently toss to coat.

20. Transfer the agnolotti to a large serving dish or individual serving bowls. Garnish with toasted pine nuts, chives, and remaining Parmigiano-Reggiano.

★

YOU CAN MAKE THE AGNOLOTTI AHEAD OF TIME AND FREEZE FOR 3 DAYS.

★

Strozzapreti with Mushrooms and Smoked Mozzarella

SERVES 4 AS A SMALL PLATE

ACTIVE TIME = 40–45 MINUTES

The word "strozzapreti" literally means "priest choker," but I promise this dish won't make you have to go to confession. The smoked mozzarella and mushrooms are the standouts in this dish.

1. Bring a large pot of salted water to a boil for the pasta. A good rule of thumb is to use 1 tablespoon of kosher salt per quart of water in your pot.

2. In a large sauté pan, heat the oils over medium-high heat. Add the mushrooms, toss to coat with oil, and season with salt. Let the mushrooms cook for 1 minute before stirring. Then, sauté for 15–20 minutes, stirring occasionally, until mushrooms are tender.

3. Add the strozzapreti to the boiling water for 10–11 minutes, or until al dente. Reserve ¼ cup of the cooking water, then drain the pasta.

4. Toss the pasta into the cooked mushrooms over medium heat. Add the reserved pasta water and butter. When the butter has melted, stir in the smoked mozzarella, Parmigiano-Reggiano, and parsley. Toss for 1–2 minutes, or until cheese has melted.

5. Transfer the pasta to a large bowl for family-style serving or individual serving bowls.

★

---

2 tablespoons canola oil

1 tablespoon extra virgin olive oil

¾ pound mixed mushroom blend (baby shiitake, oyster, maitake), stems removed

½ teaspoon kosher salt

½ pound dried strozzapreti (or any dried rolled pasta, like cavatelli)

2 tablespoons unsalted butter

1 cup small-diced smoked mozzarella (approximately ¼ pound)

1 cup grated Parmigiano-Reggiano

1 tablespoon finely chopped parsley

Chestnut Pappardelle with Rabbit, Prosciutto, and Button Mushrooms

SERVES 4 AS A SMALL PLATE

ACTIVE TIME = 1 HOUR, 45 MINUTES

———————★———————

3 cups dry white wine (Sauvignon Blanc recommended)

¾ cup sherry vinegar

1½ tablespoons plus 1 tablespoon canola oil

2 pounds rabbit legs (bone-in)

1½ teaspoons plus ½ teaspoon kosher salt

1½ cups thinly sliced onion

½ cup thinly sliced garlic

1 tablespoon tomato paste

1 cup canned crushed tomatoes

2½ cups chicken broth

1 sprig rosemary

3 sprigs thyme

2 cinnamon sticks (about 3 inches long)

(INGREDIENTS CONTINUE NEXT PAGE)

This dish is perfect when fall turns into winter, and there's a brisk chill in the air. The rabbit and prosciutto give this dish a really nice, hearty feel.

1. Preheat the oven to 325°F.

2. In a medium saucepan, bring the wine and sherry vinegar to a boil over high heat. Lower the heat to medium-high and keep on a low boil for approximately 15 minutes to reduce the liquid by half.

3. Heat 1½ tablespoons canola oil in a large heavy-bottomed pot (oven-safe) or Dutch oven over medium-high heat. Season the rabbit legs with 1½ teaspoons salt and sear on each side for 2 minutes, or until golden brown. Remove from pan and let rest at room temperature. Add the onions and garlic to the pan and sauté for 2 minutes, stirring often. Add the tomato paste and cook for 1 minute longer.

4. Add the crushed tomatoes and chicken broth to the pot and bring to a low boil. Stir in the reduced wine and vinegar mixture and keep on a low boil.

5. Place the rosemary, thyme, cinnamon sticks, and bay leaf onto a piece of cheesecloth, roll, and tie into a bundle. Add the sachet to the pot.

6. Return the seared rabbit to the pot, cover with a lid, and braise in the oven for 1 hour.

7. Place a baking rack on a baking sheet and lay the prosciutto slices on the rack without overlapping. Bake in the same oven for 10–12 minutes or until crispy and brittle to the touch. Remove and let cool at room temperature. Break the prosciutto into bite-size pieces.

8. Pull the *Chestnut Pasta Dough* into two equal pieces and flatten with the heel of your hand. Feed each piece twice through the widest setting on a pasta machine. Adjust the machine to second-widest setting and feed the dough through once. Repeat until you have reached your desired thickness. Lightly dust pasta sheets with flour and cut into 8 x 1-inch strips. Lightly dust with flour, place on a parchment-lined baking sheet, and refrigerate until ready to use.

9. Remove the rabbit from the braising liquid and let cool at room temperature until cool enough to handle.

1 bay leaf

2 ounces thinly sliced prosciutto

10 ounces *Chestnut Pasta Dough* (recipe follows)

2 cups quartered button mushrooms

2 tablespoons unsalted butter

Remove and discard the sachet bundle. Return the pot to the stove, turn the heat to medium-high, and bring to a boil. Reduce the liquid by half (this should take 20–25 minutes).

10. Gently pull the rabbit meat from the bones and add it back to the reduced liquid. Simmer for 10–12 minutes or until a rich ragu forms.

11. Bring a pot of salted water to a boil for the pasta. A good rule of thumb is to use 1 tablespoon of kosher salt per quart of water in your pot.

12. In a medium sauté pan, heat the remaining 1 tablespoon canola oil over medium-high heat. Sauté the button mushrooms for 5–7 minutes until golden brown and season with remaining ½ teaspoon salt. Stir the mushrooms into the rabbit ragu. Add butter and stir until melted.

13. Gently drop the pasta into the boiling water for 1–1½ minutes until al dente. Drain the pasta and add it to the rabbit ragu. Gently toss until the noodles are coated in sauce.

14. Transfer the parpardelle and ragu to a large serving dish or individual serving bowls and top with crispy prosciutto.

Chestnut Pasta Dough

1. Add the flours to a food processor fitted with a plastic dough blade.

2. In a separate bowl, whisk the egg yolks, water, and olive oil. Turn on the food processor and slowly add the liquid. After a minute, tiny dough balls will form. If the dough is too wet and not coming together, add a little flour. If the dough is too dry and not coming together, add a little water. It should form into one ball. Make sure you scrape down the inside of the food processor bowl to fully incorporate all the ingredients.

3. Remove the dough ball and dust with flour. Knead for 1 minute and wrap tightly in plastic wrap and refrigerate for at least 1 hour or up to 2 days. Remove from refrigerator 10 minutes before using.

MAKES APPROXIMATELY 10 OUNCES OF DOUGH

ACTIVE TIME = 5 MINUTES

INACTIVE TIME = 1 HOUR

———— ★ ————

½ cup plus 3 tablespoons "oo" flour (or all-purpose flour)

½ cup plus 3 tablespoons chestnut flour

3 large egg yolks

¼ cup water

1 teaspoon extra virgin olive oil

"oo" or all-purpose flour for dusting

———— ★ ————

YOU CAN FIND CHESTNUT FLOUR AT SPECIALTY ITALIAN MARKETS, GOURMET GROCERY STORES, OR ONLINE.

———————— ★ ————————

1 tablespoon canola oil

2 pounds duck legs (3 or 4 legs)

2 teaspoons kosher salt

1 cup thinly sliced onion

½ cup small-diced celery

¼ cup thinly sliced garlic

2 tablespoons tomato paste

½ cup dry red wine (Merlot
recommended)

2½ cups chicken broth

1 orange, quartered

1 tablespoon black peppercorns

1 tablespoon whole allspice

1 tablespoon coriander seeds

2 sprigs rosemary

2 sprigs thyme

(INGREDIENTS CONTINUE NEXT PAGE)

Cocoa Pappardelle with Braised Duck, Orange, and Spiced Coffee Jus

You might look at the title of this recipe and think, "chocolate, coffee, duck, and orange?" Trust me, the flavors all come together in a way that will blow your mind.

1. Preheat the oven to 325°F.

2. Heat the canola oil in a large heavy-bottomed pot (oven-safe) or Dutch oven over medium-high heat. Season the duck legs with salt and sear for 2 minutes on each side, or until golden brown. Remove the duck legs from the oil and let rest at room temperature.

3. Add the onions, celery, and garlic to the pot and sauté for 2 minutes, stirring often. Stir in the tomato paste and cook for 1 minute. Pour in the wine, scraping the bottom of the pot to loosen the brown bits left over from searing the duck. Simmer for 5–7 minutes, or until all the wine evaporates.

4. Add the chicken broth and orange quarters to the pot and bring to a low boil.

5. Toast the peppercorns, allspice, and coriander in a small dry sauté pan over medium heat for 5 minutes, shaking the pan often to prevent burning. Add the toasted spices to the pot, along with the rosemary, thyme, and bay leaf.

6. With the liquid at a low boil, return the seared duck to the pot, cover with a lid, and braise in the oven for 2 hours, until the duck meat is tender and falling off the bone.

7. While duck is braising, prepare the cocoa pappardelle. Divide the *Cocoa Pasta Dough* into two equal pieces and flatten them with the heel of your hand. Feed each piece twice through the widest setting on a pasta machine. Adjust the machine to the second-widest setting and feed the dough through once. Repeat until you have reached your desired thickness. Lightly dust the pasta sheets with flour and cut into 8-inch pieces.

8. Hand-cut each 8-inch piece into 1-inch-wide strips. Lightly dust with flour, place on a parchment-lined baking sheet, and refrigerate until ready to use.

9. Remove the duck from the braising liquid, and when cool enough to handle, take the meat off the bones and set it aside. Discard the bones.

10. Strain the braising liquid, discarding the solids, and return the liquid to the pot and bring it to a boil over medium-high heat. Reduce the liquid by half (this should take about 12–15 minutes).

11. Bring a pot of salted water to a boil for the pasta. A good rule of thumb is to use 1 tablespoon of kosher salt per quart of water in your pot.

12. When the strained braising liquid has reduced by half, add the brewed coffee and reduce by half again (should take about 10–12 minutes). Add the duck meat and butter to the pot and stir to incorporate.

1 bay leaf

10 ounces *Cocoa Pasta Dough* (recipe follows)

½ cup brewed strong coffee

1 tablespoon unsalted butter

½ cup baby arugula leaves, loosely packed

1 tablespoon grated Mexican chocolate or 72% dark chocolate

MAKES APPROXIMATELY 10
OUNCES OF DOUGH

ACTIVE TIME = 5 MINUTES

INACTIVE TIME = 1 HOUR

———————— ★ ————————

COCOA PASTA DOUGH

1 cup "00" flour (or all-purpose
flour), plus more for dusting

⅓ cup unsweetened cocoa powder

3 large egg yolks

¼ cup water

1 teaspoon extra virgin olive oil

13. Gently drop the pasta into the boiling water for
1–1½ minutes, until al dente. Drain the pasta, and add
to the duck. Gently toss to coat the pasta with the duck
meat and sauce.

14. Transfer everything to a large serving dish or individual serving bowls. Garnish with arugula and grated
Mexican chocolate.

Cocoa Pasta Dough

1. Add the flour and cocoa powder to a food processor
fitted with a plastic dough blade.

2. In a separate bowl, whisk the egg yolks, water, and
olive oil. Turn on the food processor and slowly add the
liquid. After a minute, tiny dough balls will form. If the
dough is too wet and not coming together, add a little
flour. If the dough is too dry and not coming together,
add a little water. It should form into one ball. Scrape
down the inside of the food processor bowl to fully incorporate all the ingredients.

3. Remove the dough ball and dust with flour. Knead
for 1 minute, wrap tightly in plastic wrap, and refrigerate for at least 1 hour or up to 2 days. Remove from refrigerator 10 minutes before using.

Egg Noodles with Spinach, Oven-Dried Tomato, and Lemon

The oven-dried tomatoes are what make this dish. You'll want those plump, warm tomatoes in every bite.

1. Preheat the oven to 225°F.

2. In a mixing bowl, toss the tomatoes with 2 teaspoons olive oil, ¼ teaspoon salt, and oregano until evenly coated.

3. Place a baking rack on a baking sheet and arrange the tomatoes flesh side up on the rack. Roast for 1½–1¾ hours. The tomatoes will shrivel but remain slightly plump in the center. Let cool at room temperature.

4. Raise the oven temperature to 375°F and bring a pot of salted water to a boil for the pasta. A good rule of thumb is to use 1 tablespoon of kosher salt per quart of water in your pot.

5. Heat the remaining 1 tablespoon olive oil in a large sauté pan over medium heat. Add the onions to the pan and sweat them for 5–6 minutes or until soft and translucent. Add the garlic and sauté for 2 minutes longer.

6. Add the spinach and ¼ teaspoon salt to the pan, tossing gently to wilt the spinach. Remove from heat, transfer to a large mixing bowl, and let cool to room temperature. Stir in the roasted tomatoes.

SERVES 4 AS A SMALL PLATE

ACTIVE TIME = 1 HOUR

INACTIVE TIME = 2 HOURS

————★————

¾ pound grape tomatoes, halved

2 teaspoons plus 1 tablespoon extra virgin olive oil

1½ teaspoons kosher salt (divided)

1 teaspoon dried oregano

1 cup small-diced onion

1 tablespoon minced garlic

5 ounces fresh baby spinach

¼ pound dried fettuccine egg noodles

2 large eggs

½ cup ricotta cheese

½ cup whole milk

¼ cup mascarpone, at room temperature

Zest of ½ lemon

1 cup plus ½ cup shredded provolone cheese

7. Add the egg noodles to the boiling water for 3–5 minutes, or until al dente. Drain, then toss noodles with the spinach mixture and let cool.

8. In a blender, purée the eggs, ricotta, milk, mascarpone, lemon zest, and remaining 1 teaspoon salt for 30–45 seconds or until smooth. Stir the purée into the spinach and noodle mixture along with 1 cup shredded provolone.

9. Transfer the mixture to a greased 8 x 8-inch baking dish and top with the remaining ½ cup shredded provolone.

10. Place the baking dish on a baking sheet in the oven for 35–40 minutes, or until the dish is heated through and the cheese is melted and bubbling. Remove from oven and let rest for 5 minutes before serving.

Pistachio Fettuccine with Lamb Ragu, Feta, and Mint

SERVES 4 AS A SMALL PLATE

ACTIVE TIME = I HOUR, 10 MINUTES

INACTIVE TIME = 3 HOURS

———————— ★ ————————

2 lamb shanks (2½–3 pounds total), bone in

1½ tablespoons kosher salt

2 teaspoons ground black pepper

3 tablespoons canola oil

1 cup small-diced onion

½ cup chopped celery

1 tablespoon minced garlic

3 cups chicken broth

2 sprigs thyme

1 bay leaf

10 ounces *Pistachio Pasta Dough* (recipe follows)

½ cup crumbled feta

2 roasted piquillo peppers, thinly sliced (found in specialty markets)

10 mint leaves, torn

¼ cup chopped roasted and salted pistachios

1 teaspoon lemon zest (about ¼ lemon)

Using nut pastes in pasta dough adds a really interesting depth of flavor, especially when you toss it with complementary sauces and herbs. The lamb and feta together with the pistachio fettucine are well balanced and delicious.

1. Preheat the oven to 325°F.

2. Season the lamb shanks with salt and pepper. Heat the canola oil in a large heavy-bottomed pot (oven-safe) or Dutch oven over medium-high heat and sear lamb shanks for 2 minutes on all sides, until golden brown. Remove lamb from the pot and let rest at room temperature.

3. Add the onion, celery, and garlic to the pot and sauté for 3–5 minutes, until the garlic is golden. Add the chicken broth, thyme, and bay leaf and bring the mixture to a low boil. Add the seared lamb shanks, cover with a lid, and braise in the oven for 3 hours, turning the shanks after 1½ hours.

4. Remove the lamb shank from the braising liquid and let cool for 15 minutes. The meat should be falling off the bone.

5. Skim any fat off the braising liquid and discard. Pass the liquid through a food mill on the smallest disk (or through a fine-mesh strainer). Discard the solids and return the liquid to the pot.

6. Take the lamb meat off the bone and shred it, discarding the fat. Return the shredded lamb to the liquid and simmer over medium heat for 10–15 minutes or until it becomes a rich stew.

7. Bring a pot of salted water to a boil for the pasta. A good rule of thumb is to use 1 tablespoon of kosher salt per quart of water in your pot.

8. Divide pistachio pasta dough into two equal pieces and flatten with the heel of your hand. Feed each piece through the widest setting on a pasta machine twice. Adjust the machine to the second-widest setting and feed the dough through once. Repeat until you have reached the fifth-widest setting or your desired thickness. Lightly dust the pasta sheets with flour and cut into 8-inch pieces.

9. Feed pasta sheets through the fettuccine cutter, and dust lightly with flour to prevent sticking.

10. Once the water is boiling, gently drop the pasta in and cook for 1–1½ minutes, until al dente. Drain the pasta and transfer it to a large serving dish or individual serving bowls. Top with lamb ragu and garnish with feta, piquillo peppers, mint leaves, pistachios, and lemon zest. You can also drizzle a bit of your favorite olive oil to finish the dish.

Pistachio Pasta Dough

1. Add the flour to a food processor fitted with the plastic dough blade.

2. In a separate bowl, whisk the egg yolks, water, pistachio paste, and olive oil. Turn on the food processor and slowly add the liquid. After a minute, tiny dough balls will form. If the dough is too wet and not coming together, add a little flour. If the dough is too dry and not coming together, add a little water. It should form into one ball. Scrape down the inside of the food processor bowl to fully incorporate all the ingredients.

3. Remove the dough ball and dust with flour. Knead for 1 minute, wrap tightly in plastic wrap, and refrigerate for at least 1 hour or up to 2 days. Remove from refrigerator 10 minutes before using.

MAKES APPROXIMATELY 10
OUNCES OF DOUGH

ACTIVE TIME = 5 MINUTES

INACTIVE TIME = 1 HOUR

———— ★ ————

1¼ cups "oo" flour (or all-purpose flour), plus more for dusting

3 large egg yolks

3 tablespoons water

1 tablespoon pistachio paste (often found in the baking aisle of the grocery store)

1 teaspoon extra virgin olive oil

Pumpkin Bucatini with Duck Liver and Golden Raisins

SERVES 4 AS A SMALL PLATE

ACTIVE TIME = 1 HOUR

———— ★ ————

10 ounces *Pumpkin Pasta Dough* **(recipe follows)**

¼ cup golden raisins

1 pound duck liver

2 tablespoons unsalted butter

1 cup small-diced shallot

½ cup bourbon

3 sage leaves, thinly sliced

———— ★ ————

USE A GOOD-QUALITY BOURBON—
I LIKE KNOB CREEK—IN THIS DISH.

Pumpkin purée starts showing up in grocery stores in October, so it's perfect for this luscious fall dish. Pumpkin and duck are meant to go together, and the plumped golden raisins add a sweet bite.

1. Line a baking sheet with parchment paper.

2. Cut the *Pumpkin Pasta Dough* into 1-inch cubes. Using a pasta extruder fitted with the bucatini attachment, place the pieces one at a time into the extruder. Bucatini will begin to form and cut at around 8 inches long. Toss with a little flour to prevent sticking, place on the baking sheet, and refrigerate. If you do not have a pasta extruder you can also use a pasta machine to create pasta sheets, then cut with the spaghetti cutter.

3. Soak the raisins in hot water for at least 10 minutes. Drain and coarsely chop.

4. Bring a pot of salted water to a boil for the pasta. A good rule of thumb is to use 1 tablespoon of kosher salt per quart of water in your pot.

5. Place the duck liver in a food processor and pulse 6–8 times, or until the liver is chopped fine.

6. In a large sauté pan, melt the butter over medium-high heat. Add the shallot and sauté for 5–7 minutes or until caramelized and golden brown, stirring often.

Add the chopped duck liver and sauté for 4–5 minutes, or until it is cooked through and browned. Add bourbon to the pan and sauté for 2–3 minutes.

7. Once the pot of water is boiling, gently drop in the pumpkin bucatini and cook for 2–2½ minutes, until al dente. Reserve ¼ cup of the cooking water before draining the bucatini. Add the reserved cooking water, pasta, raisins, and sage to the sauté pan with the duck liver.

9. Toss to coat and transfer to a large serving dish or individual serving bowls.

Pumpkin Pasta Dough

1. Add the flour to a food processor fitted with the plastic dough blade.

2. In a separate bowl, whisk the egg yolks, pumpkin purée, and olive oil. Turn on the food processor and slowly add the liquid. After a minute, tiny dough balls will form. If the dough is too wet and not coming together, add a little flour. If the dough is too dry and not coming together, add a little water. It should form into one ball. Scrape down the inside of the food processor bowl to fully incorporate all the ingredients.

3. Remove the dough ball and dust with flour. Knead for 1 minute, wrap tightly in plastic wrap, and refrigerate for at least 1 hour or up to 2 days. Remove from refrigerator 10 minutes before using.

MAKES APPROXIMATELY 10
OUNCES OF DOUGH
ACTIVE TIME = 5 MINUTES
INACTIVE TIME = 1 HOUR

———————★———————

PUMPKIN PASTA DOUGH

1¼ cups "00" flour (or all-purpose flour), plus more for dusting

3 large egg yolks

¼ cup pumpkin purée (canned)

1 teaspoon extra virgin olive oil

Lemon Fettuccine with Bottarga and Chive

SERVES 4 AS A SMALL PLATE

ACTIVE TIME = 25–30 MINUTES

———————★———————

10 ounces *Lemon Pasta Dough* (recipe follows)

3 tablespoons unsalted butter

1 teaspoon lemon juice

3 tablespoons plus 1 tablespoon grated Parmigiano-Reggiano

2 tablespoons plus 1 tablespoon grated bottarga

1 tablespoon finely chopped chives

Freshly cracked black pepper

Bottarga is a dense, cured mullet roe that's been pressed into a hard block. It's salty, briny, tastes a little bit like caviar, and adds an almost silky texture to your finished dish. In terms of flavor, a little of it goes a long way. You can find bottarga at grocery stores where they sell smoked fish or at Italian specialty markets, or you can order it online.

1. Bring a large pot of salted water to a boil. A good rule of thumb is to use 1 tablespoon of kosher salt per quart of water in your pot.

2. Divide the *Lemon Pasta Dough* into two equal pieces and flatten with the heel of your hand. Feed each piece through the widest setting on a pasta machine twice. Adjust the rollers one setting closer together and feed the dough through once. Repeat, decreasing the thickness each time until you have fed the dough through five separate times.

3. Lightly dust the pasta sheets with flour and cut them into 8-inch-long pieces. Feed the pasta through the fettuccine cutter and toss the pasta lightly with flour to prevent sticking.

4. Drop pasta into boiling water for 1–1½ minutes, until al dente. Drain the fettucine, reserving ¼ cup of the cooking water.

5. Melt the butter in a large sauté pan over medium heat. Toss the fettuccine with melted butter, reserved cooking water, and lemon juice. Add 3 tablespoons Parmigiano-Reggiano and 2 tablespoons bottarga. Toss to coat.

6. Transfer the fettucine to a large serving dish or individual serving bowls and garnish with remaining Parmigiano-Reggiano and bottarga, chives, and a few turns of cracked black pepper.

Lemon Pasta Dough

MAKES APPROXIMATELY 10
OUNCES OF DOUGH

ACTIVE TIME = 10 MINUTES

INACTIVE TIME = 1 HOUR

———————— ★ ————————

1¼ cups "00" flour (or all-purpose
flour), plus more for dusting

3 large egg yolks

¼ cup water

1 tablespoon lemon zest (about 1
lemon)

1 teaspoon extra virgin olive oil

1. Add flour to a food processor fitted with a plastic dough blade.

2. In a separate bowl, whisk the egg yolks, water, lemon zest, and olive oil. Turn on the food processor and slowly add the liquid. After a minute, tiny dough balls will form. If the dough is too wet and not coming together, add a little flour. If the dough is too dry and not coming together, add a little water. It should form into one ball. Scrape down the inside of the food processor bowl to fully incorporate all the ingredients.

3. Remove the dough ball and dust with flour. Knead for 1 minute, wrap tightly in plastic wrap, and refrigerate for at least 1 hour or up to 2 days. Remove from refrigerator 10 minutes before using.

Red Wine–Stained Angel Hair with Octopus Ragu

Serving spaghetti or angel hair pasta cooked in red wine is not only visually appealing, it tastes like nothing else. This pasta almost doesn't need any sauce, but I can't resist serving it with octopus. The octopus breaks down into the ragu and releases its own liquid into the sauce.

1. Grind frozen octopus using a coarse meat grinder. Set aside to thaw. *If you do not have a grinder, don't freeze the octopus and instead chop it into a ¼-inch dice. This will take more time than noted above.

2. Heat ¼ cup olive oil in a large, heavy-bottomed pot over high heat and sauté the octopus for 3 minutes, stirring occasionally. The meat will release a little moisture into the pan.

3. Stir in the onions, garlic, and bay leaf and sauté 3 minutes longer, or until the onions are soft and translucent. Add the crushed tomatoes, oregano, and chili flakes. Bring the mixture to a low boil and reduce the heat to low. Simmer uncovered for 45 minutes, stirring every 10 minutes. The liquid will reduce and the octopus will become tender.

4. Bring a pot of salted water to a boil for the pasta. A good rule of thumb is to use 1 tablespoon of kosher salt per quart of water in your pot.

SERVES 4 AS A SMALL PLATE
ACTIVE TIME = 1 HOUR, 15 MINUTES

———— ★ ————

1¼ pounds octopus tentacles, cut into 1-inch cubes and frozen (see Step 1)

¼ cup plus 1 teaspoon extra virgin olive oil

⅓ cup small-diced onion

1 tablespoon minced garlic

1 bay leaf

½ cup canned crushed tomatoes

¼ teaspoon dried oregano

¼ teaspoon red chili flakes

6 ounces dried angel hair pasta

1 750ml bottle red wine (Merlot recommended)

1 tablespoon sugar

1 tablespoon finely chopped chives

5. Boil the angel hair pasta for just 1½ minutes—it will not be fully cooked. Drain and set aside.

6. Return the empty pasta pot to the stove and add the red wine and sugar. Bring to a boil over high heat. Lower the heat to medium and simmer for 10–12 minutes, or until wine reduces by half. At this point the octopus ragu should be finished and can be kept warm on the stove until pasta is ready.

7. Return the reduced wine to a boil and add the pasta to finish cooking it. Gently stir the pasta to prevent sticking and boil for 1½ minutes, until the pasta is al dente. Drain and toss the pasta with remaining olive oil to prevent sticking, then transfer to a large bowl or individual bowls and top with the octopus ragu. Garnish with chives and serve.

8 the shell game

MY FIRST SEASON on *Top Chef* was brutal, although I loved being in the same cast as my friends Bryan and Michael Voltaggio. Some of those competitions and challenges were rough, I'm not gonna lie, and don't even get me started on the Judges' Table. Though it's only a few minutes on TV, the whole Judges' Table process can last up to 7 hours, and even when you know you cooked a great dish, it's exhausting. The Quickfire Challenges, on the other hand, where you don't have much time to cook, were totally energizing. They're as close to live television as you can get. I liked the Quickfires because you really only have 5 minutes, tops, to think about what you're going to make after you've heard the rules. Your instincts kick in and the adrenaline pushes you through. It really levels the playing field and lets a chef's true talents shine.

Being on *Top Chef All-Stars* was a little different because we'd all been there before, so there wasn't much the judges could do that we wouldn't expect or know how to handle. And while the Elimination Challenges were interesting on both seasons I did the show, I think my favorite was the Ellis Island challenge, where we had to come up with a dish based on our heritage. To be able to see my family and cook from my heart was something I knew I had to do to make it to the finals. The Ellis Island episode is where I also learned that my competitor, Antonia Lofaso, was a distant cousin, which made for an even more friendly competition and lifelong friendship. The "Not My Cousin's Mussels" recipe in this chapter is a shout-out to her.

Growing up on the East Coast, eating shellfish was pretty common. I learned the "real" way to prepare shellfish in culinary school, and as I learned under my chef mentors I refined my technique. Shellfish is a staple in Italian and Mediterranean cooking, and it's important to use really fresh ingredients when making these recipes. Find a fishmonger or good fish and seafood purveyor in your area and get to know them so they'll order the freshest, best shellfish for you.

Not My Cousin's Mussels

On Top Chef All-Stars, *one of our challenges took place at Rao's, a New York institution when it comes to classical, old-school Italian cooking. My sort-of cousin and co-cheftestant, Antonia Lofaso, won that intensely Italian-focused challenge with what sounded a lot like a French preparation of mussels. This recipe is a tribute to her and her winning dish. No hard feelings, cousin.*

1. Heat the canola oil in a large saucepan over medium-high heat. Add the shallots, peppercorns, and parsley sprigs and sauté for 2–3 minutes. Evenly distribute saffron threads into the pan.

2. Add the mussels to the pan and pour in the wine. Immediately cover and steam mussels for 4–5 minutes. Discard any that do not open.

3. Pour the mussels and the cooking liquid through a small fine-mesh strainer over a bowl, reserving the liquid. Remove mussels from their shells and refrigerate. Discard the shells and other solids.

4. In a large mixing bowl, whisk ¼ cup of reserved mussel liquid, olive oil, lemon juice, salt, and black pepper. Toss with fennel, grape tomatoes, celery, and the chilled mussels.

5. Arrange the mussel salad on a serving platter and garnish with pistachios and parsley. Serve immediately.

SERVES 4 AS A SMALL PLATE

ACTIVE TIME = 20–25 MINUTES

———— ★ ————

1 tablespoon canola oil

¼ cup small-diced shallots

1 teaspoon whole black peppercorns

10 sprigs fresh parsley

¼ teaspoon saffron threads

1 pound mussels, cleaned and debearded

½ cup white wine

2 tablespoons extra virgin olive oil

1 tablespoon lemon juice

¼ teaspoon kosher salt

¼ teaspoon freshly cracked black pepper

2 cups thinly shaved fennel

1½ cups grape tomatoes, halved

1 cup thinly sliced celery

½ cup chopped roasted and salted pistachios

¼ cup torn parsley leaves

Clam Bake with Braised Kale and Pancetta Crumbs

SERVES 4 AS A SMALL PLATE

ACTIVE TIME = 50–60 MINUTES

———— ★ ————

BRAISED KALE

3 tablespoons extra virgin olive oil

1 shallot, minced

2 garlic cloves, minced

3 cups thinly sliced kale, stems removed

1 cup chicken broth

1 teaspoon lemon juice

PANCETTA CRUMBS

1 tablespoon extra virgin olive oil

¼ cup finely diced pancetta

½ cup panko bread crumbs

1 tablespoon finely chopped parsley

1 tablespoon lemon zest

1 teaspoon ground red chili flakes

¼ teaspoon salt

(INGREDIENTS CONTINUE NEXT PAGE)

Every summer, when we visited my extended family in Jones Beach, there would be a big grill set up in the sand, and my uncles would try to outdo each other in a cook-off. One thing I remember them making was grilled clams, and this dish is a tribute to them. It's an updated version of clams casino, where I use braised kale because I like the richness it brings to the dish. You'll want the pancetta crumbs to be golden brown on top. This way, the clams cook through but aren't overdone.

1. Heat 2 tablespoons of olive oil in a large sauté pan over medium-low heat and sweat the shallot and garlic for 5–6 minutes, until soft. Stir in the chopped kale and cook for an additional 4 minutes, stirring every so often to help wilt the kale.

2. Add the chicken broth and bring to a low boil. Reduce heat and cover the pan, leaving a slight opening, and gently simmer for 45 minutes.

3. Prepare the pancetta bread crumbs: heat the olive oil in a large sauté pan over medium heat and sauté the pancetta for 5 minutes, or until crispy. Reserving the fat, remove the cooked pancetta and drain on a paper towel. Chop the cooked pancetta into smaller pieces to match the size of the bread crumbs.

4. Add the bread crumbs to the pancetta fat. Sauté over medium heat for 4–5 minutes, until they become light brown. Remove from the heat and let the bread crumbs cool in the pan. Stir in pancetta, parsley, lemon zest, chili flakes, and salt.

5. Preheat the oven to 450°F.

6. Heat a large sauté pan over medium-high heat for 2–3 minutes. When the pan is hot, add the garlic, clams, and white wine. Cover immediately and allow clams to steam open. This should take no more than a minute.

7. Remove pan from heat, checking to make sure all the clams have opened. Discard any clams that remain closed. Carefully twist off the top shell and, using a paring knife, gently loosen the clam from the bottom shell. Keeping the clam in the bottom shell, evenly line them on a baking sheet. If you need to, you can use rock salt to hold the shells in place.

8. Slightly drain the kale and stir in the remaining tablespoon of olive oil and lemon juice.

9. Top each clam with a teaspoon each of braised kale and pancetta bread crumbs. Bake for 10 minutes. Serve immediately.

CLAMS

4 cloves garlic, smashed

24 middleneck clams

½ cup white wine

———— ★ ————

THE BRAISED KALE AND PANCETTA BREAD CRUMBS CAN BE PREPARED ONE DAY IN ADVANCE.

---------- ★ ----------

12 large head-on prawns, peeled and deveined

¼ teaspoon plus ¼ teaspoon salt

12 large Thai basil leaves (24 if small)

12 slices cured lardo, 6 inches long

1 tablespoon canola oil

2 tablespoons extra virgin olive oil

1 tablespoon lemon juice

1½ cups thinly shaved fennel

1 tablespoon finely chopped fennel fronds

1 cup *Tomato Pesto* (page 37)

---------- ★ ----------

YOU CAN WRAP THE PRAWNS AND REFRIGERATE FOR UP TO A DAY AHEAD OF TIME. SEAR RIGHT BEFORE SERVING.

Lardo-Wrapped Prawns with Tomato Pesto and Fennel Salad

What I love about this dish is that the natural fat of the lardo actually helps cook the prawns for you. I use Thai basil in this dish instead of Italian sweet basil because Thai basil's anise-like flavor works with the fennel and holds its flavor better. Use a mandoline to slice the fennel as thinly as you can. If you can't find prawns, it's okay to substitute jumbo shrimp.

Lardo is a special cut of a pig's "fatback" flavored with herbs and spices and cured in a salty brine. You can find lardo in an Italian specialty market or with other cured meats and hams at the grocery store.

1. Season the prawns with ¼ teaspoon salt.

2. Wrap 1–2 (depending on size) Thai basil leaves around each prawn. Then, wrap each prawn with a slice of lardo, making sure to fully cover each prawn.

3. Heat the canola oil in a large sauté pan over medium-high heat and sear prawns for 2 minutes on each side. The lardo will melt away.

4. Whisk together the olive oil, lemon juice, and remaining ¼ teaspoon salt to make a vinaigrette. Toss with the shaved fennel and fennel fronds.

5. Serve the lardo-wrapped prawns over the fennel salad with the *Tomato Pesto* on the side.

Oysters with Blood Orange, Crème Fraîche, and Radish

SERVES 4 AS A SMALL PLATE,
WITH 4 OYSTERS PER PERSON
ACTIVE TIME = 45 MINUTES

———— ★ ————

¼ cup crème fraîche

2 teaspoons blood orange zest

1 teaspoon blood orange juice

1 teaspoon extra virgin olive oil

⅛ teaspoon kosher salt

4 radishes

16 East Coast oysters (Beausoleil recommended)

8 blood orange segments, supremed (page 39) and cut in half

———— ★ ————

YOU CAN HAVE THE PERSON AT YOUR FISH COUNTER SHUCK THE OYSTERS FOR YOU. JUST KEEP ALL THE BOTTOM SHELLS AND THE OYSTER LIQUOR.

When my wife, Stacy, and I go out to eat, I like to start off dinner with a round of fresh oysters. A traditional mignonette is fine, but I wanted to come up with a different, slightly sweet, acidic, and peppery complement when I offered oysters at Graffiato. That's where the crème fraîche, orange, and radish come in. It not only bolsters the sweet, briny flavor of the oysters, but the added crunch from the radish gives it some texture.

1. Combine the crème fraîche, blood orange zest, blood orange juice, olive oil and salt in a mixing bowl. Stir, cover, and refrigerate for 20–30 minutes.

2. Slice each radish into ⅛-inch rounds, then slice each round into ⅛-inch sticks.

3. Shuck the oysters by gripping each one in a kitchen towel and, using an oyster knife, finding the small opening between the shells near the hinge and twisting the knife to open. Cut the oyster loose from the top shell and discard. Loosen the oyster from the bottom shell with the knife and keep the oyster and its juices (also called "liquor") in the bottom shell for serving.

4. Place oysters on a serving platter, using rock salt to keep the shells in place. Dollop the crème fraîche mixture onto each oyster. Garnish with radish sticks and blood orange pieces. Serve immediately.

Scallop Crudo with Grapefruit, Black Pepper Yogurt, and Caviar

Buy the freshest scallops you can find and make sure your knife is sharp when slicing them into discs. This is a really beautiful dish in its presentation, and the grapefruit with the caviar and black pepper yogurt add an artful balance.

1. Slice each scallop across, horizontally, into four discs. Gently toss scallops in a glass or other nonreactive mixing bowl with 1 tablespoon olive oil and salt. Cover and marinate in the refrigerator for 30 minutes.

2. In a separate bowl, combine the yogurt, grapefruit zest and juice, 1 teaspoon olive oil, and black pepper. Refrigerate for at least 20 minutes.

3. Arrange the scallop discs on a serving dish. Dollop yogurt mixture onto each piece, and top each with ⅛ teaspoon caviar and grapefruit pieces. Serve immediately.

SERVES 4 AS A SMALL PLATE
ACTIVE TIME = 15 MINUTES
INACTIVE TIME = 50 MINUTES

———— ★ ————

6 scallops (U10 or U12)

1 tablespoon plus 1 teaspoon extra virgin olive oil

¼ teaspoon kosher salt

¼ cup plain Greek yogurt

2 teaspoons grapefruit zest

1 teaspoon grapefruit juice

¼ teaspoon freshly cracked black pepper

1 ounce American paddlefish caviar

6 supremed grapefruit segments (page 39), cut in quarters

Razor Clams Scapece

SERVES 4 AS A SMALL PLATE

ACTIVE TIME = 1 HOUR

INACTIVE TIME = 20–25 MINUTES

———— ★ ————

1 red bell pepper, lightly oiled with extra virgin olive oil and seasoned with salt

½ cup extra virgin olive oil

3 tablespoons sherry vinegar

¼ cup finely shaved red onion

2 tablespoons finely chopped parsley

1 teaspoon minced garlic

1 teaspoon kosher salt

3 tablespoons canola oil

20 razor clams

———— ★ ————

THREE TABLESPOONS FINELY DICED JARRED ROASTED RED PEPPERS CAN BE SUBSTITUTED FOR ROASTING YOUR OWN.

A traditional scapece is poached or fried fish in a spicy marinade, refrigerated for 24 hours, and served cold. This dish is a riff on the traditional in that it combines a flavorful marinade with one of my favorite shellfish: razor clams. Razor clams are a meaty clam: sweet like scallops and resembling the texture of baby squid. A fresh razor clam will have extended itself outside the shell and will retract when picked up. It's always best to cook razor clams the day you buy them.

1. Preheat the oven broiler on high.

2. Place the pepper on a baking sheet and broil for 5 minutes on each side until nice and charred all around. Place the charred pepper in a glass bowl, cover with plastic wrap, and set aside for 20 minutes.

3. In a separate glass bowl, combine the olive oil and sherry vinegar. Stir in onion, parsley, garlic, and salt.

4. Peel the cooled pepper with a paring knife and remove and discard the ribs and seeds. Finely dice and stir into the onion mixture. Let rest at room temperature for 30 minutes.

5. Rinse the clams under cool, running water. Pry them open with a paring knife and remove meat from shell. Using kitchen scissors, snip off the dark siphon at the top of the clam and cut open the body from the tip to

the base. Remove the dark gills, digger, and stomach. This will leave you with a butterflied-open clam with all the dark parts removed.

6. Heat the canola oil in a large sauté pan over medium-high heat. Sear razor clams on one side for 2 minutes, then flip them over, drizzle with half the onion mixture, and cook for another minute.

7. Stack the clams on a serving platter and garnish with the remaining onion mixture. Serve immediately.

————★————

FRESH RAZOR CLAMS SHOULD SMELL LIKE THE SEA, BUT NOT SMELL FISHY OR LIKE AMMONIA.

————★————

Lobster Risotto with Preserved Lemon

SERVES 4 AS A SMALL PLATE

ACTIVE TIME = 35–40 MINUTES

INACTIVE TIME = 40 MINUTES

———— ★ ————

2 tablespoons distilled white vinegar

1 live, 2-pound lobster

3 tablespoons canola oil

1 cup small-diced onion

1 cup small-diced carrots

¼ cup diced garlic

4 sprigs thyme

2 tablespoons tomato paste

1 teaspoon kosher salt

1 quart water

1 tablespoon butter

¼ cup small-diced shallots

1 cup carnaroli short-grain rice

1 tablespoon small-diced preserved lemon

Kosher salt to taste

2 tablespoons small-diced bone marrow or butter

5 leaves basil, torn or chiffonade

Lobster risotto is rich, but preserved lemon cuts through that richness and boosts the flavor profile of this dish. I prefer using carnaroli rice for risotto because carnaroli contains a little more starch (which is what gives risotto its creamy texture) and retains liquid better than Arborio rice. Carnaroli rice holds its shape better and has a larger grain, which gives it that perfect toothiness you want in risotto. You can find preserved lemon in most grocery stores—sometimes in a jar in the jam section, and other times at the olive bar in the deli section.

1. Fill a small stockpot with water two-thirds full, bring to a boil, and add the vinegar. Set a bowl of ice water to the side.

2. Quickly twist off the claws and tail from the live lobster.

3. Drop the claws into the boiling water for 1 minute, then add the tail and cook for an additional 2 minutes. Using tongs, remove tail and claws from the boiling water and shock in ice water to stop cooking.

4. Lift up and pull off the uncooked lobster body shell and remove and discard all innards and gills.

5. Holding the body, twist and remove the small legs and cut the body into quarters.

6. To make the lobster stock, heat the canola oil in a large stockpot over medium-high heat. Add lobster body pieces, small legs, and body shell to the pot and cook for 5 minutes, stirring occasionally.

7. Add the onions, carrots, garlic, and thyme and sauté for 8–10 minutes or until lightly browned.

8. Stir in the tomato paste and cook for 2 minutes. Season with salt, then add the water. Increase heat to bring the mixture to a boil. Reduce heat to low, cover, and simmer for 40 minutes.

9. Remove the lobster claws and tail from the cold water. Using kitchen scissors or a sharp knife, cut open the shells and remove the meat, which should be slightly undercooked. Dice the claw and tail meat into ¾-inch pieces. Cover with plastic wrap and refrigerate.

10. Remove the lobster stock from the heat and let cool slightly. Take out the lobster shell and legs and discard. Pass the liquid through a food mill, then through a fine-mesh strainer three times. This should yield 3 cups of stock. If not, add a little hot water to bring it up to 3 cups. Keep the lobster stock warm in a saucepan over medium heat.

11. In a separate large, heavy-bottomed pot over medium heat, melt the butter. Add the shallots and sweat them for 4–5 minutes, or until soft and tender. You do not want any color. Add the carnaroli rice and stir for 3–4 minutes to start the risotto.

12. Add lobster stock to the risotto ½ cup at a time and continually stir the rice in one direction. When stock has been absorbed, add another ½ cup and continue to

stir in the same direction. Repeat until all but the last ½ cup of stock has been used.

13. With the last ½ cup of stock, also stir in the preserved lemon and lobster meat. Continue stirring in one direction, and cook for 2 minutes. Season with salt to taste.

14. Add the bone marrow, stirring to melt it into the risotto.

15. Transfer the lobster risotto to a serving dish and garnish with basil leaves.

Scallop Cutlets with Bacon Bread Crumbs and Arugula Pesto

SERVES 4 AS A SMALL PLATE

ACTIVE TIME = 30–40 MINUTES

———————————★———————————

6 scallops (U10 or U12)

1 tablespoon pine nuts

1 tablespoon plus ½ cup extra virgin olive oil

3 slices thick-cut bacon (¼-inch thick)

1½ cups panko bread crumbs

1½ tablespoons finely chopped chives

½ teaspoon kosher salt

¼ cup all-purpose flour

1 large egg, beaten

¼ cup torn arugula leaves, lightly packed

⅔ cup *Arugula Pesto* (recipe follows)

1 lemon, quartered

It seems like every wedding reception you go to, there are trays of bacon-wrapped scallops being passed, and they're usually pretty bland and gross. This recipe takes that concept and turns it on its head, blowing the flavors wide open.

1. Slice the scallops in half, horizontally, creating two discs per scallop. Place each disc between two sheets of plastic wrap and, using a flat mallet, very gently pound them to about ⅛ inch thick. Keep covered with plastic wrap and refrigerate.

2. Toast the pine nuts in a dry sauté pan for 5 minutes, shaking the pan often to prevent burning.

3. Heat 1 tablespoon of olive oil in a medium sauté pan over medium heat. Add the bacon and sauté for 8 minutes, until crispy. Keeping the fat in the pan, remove the cooked bacon and drain on a paper towel. Mince the bacon.

4. Add the bread crumbs to the bacon fat and sauté over medium heat for 2–3 minutes. If the bread crumbs begin to brown, remove from heat. Transfer the bread crumbs to a mixing bowl and let cool. Stir in the bacon, chives, and salt.

5. Set up the breading station with three separate shallow bowls for flour, egg, and bacon bread crumbs.

6. Dredge each scallop disc in flour, then egg, then bread crumbs. Patting the bread crumbs on the scallop will ensure they stick.

7. Heat ½ cup of olive oil in a large sauté pan over medium-high heat. In small batches, fry the scallops for 1 minute on each side until golden brown. If the breading browns too quickly, lower the heat to medium.

8. Remove scallops from the pan and place on a cooling rack or paper towels to drain. Arrange the scallops on a serving dish and garnish with pine nuts and torn arugula leaves. Serve with *Arugula Pesto* and lemon quarters on the side.

Arugula Pesto

1. In a food processor, combine the arugula, Parmigiano-Reggiano, pine nuts, garlic, and salt.

2. Turn on the processor and slowly add the olive oil until a paste forms, approximately 1 minute.

MAKES APPROXIMATELY ⅔ CUP
ACTIVE TIME = 10–12 MINUTES

------------ ★ ------------

ARUGULA PESTO

2 cups chopped baby arugula, tightly packed

¼ cup grated Parmigiano-Reggiano

2 tablespoons pine nuts, toasted

1 teaspoon minced garlic

½ teaspoon kosher salt

⅓ cup extra virgin olive oil

------------ ★ ------------

PESTO CAN BE REFRIGERATED FOR UP TO 3 DAYS.

Steamed Mussels with Pancetta, Yuengling, and Goat Cheese

SERVES 4 AS A SMALL PLATE

ACTIVE TIME = 40–45 MINUTES

———————★———————

1 tablespoon canola oil

½ cup finely diced pancetta

½ cup thinly sliced shallot rings

2 tablespoons whole-grain mustard

2 pounds mussels, cleaned and debearded

1 cup Yuengling lager (or the amber lager of your choice)

2 ounces goat cheese, crumbled

1 tablespoon finely chopped chives

Traditionally, mussels are steamed in wine. They're delicious that way, don't get me wrong. That said, I like mine steamed in beer, and I really like them steamed in Yuengling. If you can't find Yuengling where you live, use whatever amber lager you prefer. The mussels with the beer make for a delicious broth that you won't want to leave in the bowl when you're done, so have some slices of grilled or toasted ciabatta nearby to finish this off.

1. Heat the canola oil in a large saucepan over medium-high heat. Add the pancetta and crisp for 3 minutes, stirring occasionally. Add shallots and sweat them for 2 minutes. Stir in the mustard and sauté 1 minute longer.

2. Add the mussels to the pan and pour in the beer. Immediately cover the pan and steam the mussels for 4–5 minutes. Pick out and discard any that do not open.

3. Pour the mussels and liquid into a large serving bowl and top with goat cheese and chives. Serve immediately.

9 gone fishing

EVERY SUMMER WHEN I was growing up, my dad would take my cousins and me fishing on the waters off Long Island. We'd catch fluke, bluefish, tuna, and striped bass, and then we'd take them back to my cousin's beach house to clean them and cook them. I have really fond memories of the smell of fish on the grill mixed with the salt air, and fresh summer salads on the table. Whether we ate it grilled with lemon juice or whole roasted with juicy, ripe tomatoes, fish was a staple every summer and something that always reminds me of family.

When *Top Chef All-Stars* had us go out fishing in those same waters, I had a blast. Being in a boat with Richie, Fabio, and Angelo was a lot of fun—it felt like being home. And, landing in the winners' circle that night made it all the more special. Even though I didn't ultimately win, I felt like I really showed who I am with my food that night.

Today, I make a point of going fishing out on the Chesapeake Bay whenever I can. I like to take my sous chefs and line cooks with me so they can have a feel for where our ingredients come from.

I encourage you to take the time to find a fishmonger or an excellent seafood market near you where you can get your hands on fish the day it's caught, or the day after. That's when it's best. Some fish is flash-frozen immediately after it's caught, and that's great to use, too. Good fish shouldn't smell fishy at all; it should smell fresh.

Bluefish Scapece with Olive Oil–Smashed Potatoes and Red Peppers

SERVES 4 AS A SMALL PLATE

ACTIVE TIME = 1 HOUR

———— ★ ————

MARINADE

1 teaspoon black peppercorns

1 teaspoon whole allspice

1½ cups water

1 cup sherry vinegar

½ cup light brown sugar

½ cup rough-chopped red bell pepper

¼ cup thinly sliced shallot

2 sprigs thyme

1 bay leaf

1 cinnamon stick (2 inches long)

BLUEFISH

1 tablespoon coriander seeds

1 teaspoon fennel seeds

1 teaspoon black peppercorns

½ teaspoon whole allspice

½ teaspoon kosher salt

(INGREDIENTS CONTINUE NEXT PAGE)

Bluefish has an undeserved bad rap—it's often referred to as "trash fish," which it's not. When it's fresh, bluefish is phenomenal. It's clean, it's white, it's solid—in fact, it's one of my favorite fish. The key to using bluefish is to cook it the day or day after it's caught. This dish is based on a traditional escabeche in that it combines the fish with a flavorful marinade.

1. To prepare the marinade, toast the peppercorns and allspice in a dry sauté pan over medium heat for 5 minutes, shaking the pan often to prevent burning. In a medium saucepan, combine the toasted spices and all the other ingredients for the marinade. Bring to a boil, cover, and remove from the heat. Let steep for 15 minutes, then strain, reserving the liquids and discarding the solids.

2. To prepare the bluefish, toast the coriander, fennel seeds, peppercorns, and allspice in a dry sauté pan over medium heat for 5 minutes, shaking the pan often to prevent burning. Transfer to a spice grinder along with the salt and red chili flakes and grind into a fine powder. Rub the bluefish filets with the spice powder.

3. Heat the canola oil in a large sauté pan over high heat and fry the bluefish filets on one side for 3 minutes, flip,

and cook 2 minutes longer. Transfer the bluefish to a deep baking dish and pour the marinade over the fish, submerging it fully, and let it marinate at room temperature for 20 minutes.

4. To prepare the smashed potatoes, place the potatoes in a medium saucepan, cover with water, and add 1 teaspoon salt. Bring to a boil for 10–12 minutes, or until the potatoes are fork tender.

5. To prepare the garnish, in a small mixing bowl, stir together all the garnish ingredients.

6. Drain the potatoes and place in a large mixing bowl. Add the olive oil and remaining ½ teaspoon salt. Smash with a fork or potato masher until all ingredients are incorporated.

7. Arrange the potatoes on a serving dish. Remove the bluefish from the marinade and place on top of the potatoes. Garnish with the red pepper salad and serve at room temperature.

¼ teaspoon red chili flakes

1 pound cleaned bluefish filet, skin removed, cut into 4 equal portions

2 tablespoons canola oil

POTATOES

1 pound golden baby potatoes

1 teaspoon plus ½ teaspoon kosher salt

⅓ cup extra virgin olive oil

GARNISH

½ cup thinly shaved red bell pepper

2 radishes, thinly shaved

4 teaspoons chopped dill

4 teaspoons extra virgin olive oil

½ teaspoon sea salt (Maldon recommended)

———————— ★ ————————

USE A MANDOLINE TO SLICE THE BELL PEPPERS AND RADISHES FOR THE MARINADE

Olive Oil–Poached Cod with Squash Blossom Pesto

SERVES 4 AS A SMALL PLATE

ACTIVE TIME = 25–30 MINUTES

———————★———————

1 quart extra virgin olive oil

1 sprig thyme

1 bay leaf

1 clove garlic, smashed

Peel of ½ lemon (no pith)

1-pound cod filet, skin removed, cut into 4 equal portions

2 teaspoons kosher salt

¼ cup canola oil

1 tablespoon cornstarch

1 tablespoon water

8 squash blossom petals (from 2–3 squash blossoms)

¼ teaspoon sea salt

¾ cup *Squash Blossom Pesto* (recipe follows)

———————★———————

USE A SHARP VEGETABLE PEELER TO REMOVE THE THIN PEEL OF THE LEMON.

Cod is a popular mild, white fish. It's lean and flaky and handles olive oil poaching better than almost any other fish. The squash blossom pesto is the perfect accompaniment.

1. In a large, heavy-bottomed pot, bring olive oil, thyme, bay leaf, garlic, and lemon peel to 170°F. Clip a candy thermometer onto the inside of the pot to measure the oil's temperature.

2. Season the cod filets with salt and poach in the hot olive oil for 6–8 minutes or until fully cooked. Use a cake tester to check doneness: it should slide out easily with no resistance, and the end should be warm to the touch.

3. Heat the canola oil in a sauté pan over medium-high heat.

4. In a small bowl, whisk together cornstarch and water. Lightly brush each squash blossom petal on both sides with this mixture.

5. Pan-fry each petal for 30–45 seconds on each side or until lightly golden and crispy. Drain on paper towels and season with sea salt.

6. Spoon *Squash Blossom Pesto* onto a serving dish. Use a slotted spoon to remove the cod from the oil and place on top of the pesto. Garnish with crispy petals and serve immediately.

Squash Blossom Pesto

1. Bring a medium saucepan of salted water to a boil. Set a bowl of ice water to the side. When the water is at a full boil, add the saffron threads and yellow squash and blanch for 1 minute. Remove the squash from the boiling water with a slotted spoon and shock it in the ice water.

2. Keeping the water boiling, blanch squash blossom petals for 30 seconds and shock in the ice water. Remove the squash and petals from the water and pat dry with paper towels or a clean dishtowel.

3. Toast the pine nuts in a dry sauté pan over medium heat for 5 minutes, shaking the pan often to prevent burning.

4. In a food processor, combine the squash, squash blossom petals, toasted pine nuts, Pecorino, and salt. While the processor is running, slowly add olive oil until a paste forms, approximately 30–45 seconds.

MAKES APPROXIMATELY ¾ CUP
ACTIVE TIME = 20 MINUTES

————★————

6 threads saffron

½ cup small-diced yellow squash

Petals from 6 squash blossoms

2 tablespoons pine nuts

¼ cup grated Pecorino

¼ teaspoon kosher salt

¼ cup extra virgin olive oil

————★————

PESTO CAN BE REFRIGERATED FOR UP TO 3 DAYS.

Seared Bigeye Tuna with Eggplant Caponata

SERVES 4 AS A SMALL PLATE

ACTIVE TIME = 1 HOUR

———————— ★ ————————

1 small red bell pepper, lightly brushed with olive oil and seasoned with salt

¼ cup golden raisins

3 tablespoons pine nuts

10 tablespoons canola oil (divided)

1 medium eggplant, cut into ½-inch cubes (about 2 cups)

2 teaspoons curry powder

1½ teaspoons kosher salt (divided)

½ cup medium-diced red onion

½ cup medium-diced zucchini

½ cup medium-diced yellow squash

1 tablespoon capers

2 tablespoons extra virgin olive oil

2 tablespoons balsamic vinegar

1 pound bigeye tuna loin; center cut

¼ teaspoon sea salt (Maldon recommended)

Caponata is an Italian, sweet-and-sour version of ratatouille. It complements a bold-tasting fish like tuna and is actually really good on its own on top of toast, if you have any left over. You could make the eggplant caponata a day before serving this dish and let it set up in the refrigerator overnight to allow the flavors to become even more pronounced.

1. Preheat the oven broiler on high.

2. Place the pepper on its side on a baking sheet. Broil for 5 minutes on each side to char the skin and soften the flesh. Place in a glass bowl and cover tightly with plastic wrap. Let cool for 20 minutes.

3. Steep the raisins in a bowl of hot water for 15–20 minutes to plump and soften them. Strain and set aside.

4. Toast pine nuts in a dry sauté pan for 5 minutes, shaking the pan often to prevent burning. Place the toasted pine nuts in a large mixing bowl.

5. Heat 5 tablespoons canola oil in a large sauté pan over medium heat. Add the eggplant, curry powder, and ¼ teaspoon salt. Toss to coat and sauté for 6–7 minutes or until eggplant is tender. Transfer the cooked eggplant to the mixing bowl with the pine nuts.

6. Add 1½ tablespoons canola oil to the same sauté pan over medium heat. Sweat the red onions with ¼ teaspoon salt for 2–3 minutes or until soft and translucent. Transfer to the same mixing bowl.

7. Add another 1½ tablespoons canola oil to the same pan over medium heat again. Sauté the zucchini, squash, and ¼ teaspoon salt for 5 minutes, or until tender. Transfer to the same mixing bowl.

8. Take the charred red pepper and remove and discard the skin, ribs, and seeds. Finely dice the bell pepper flesh and add it to a mixing bowl with other vegetables. Stir in the golden raisins, capers, olive oil, balsamic vinegar, and ¼ teaspoon salt. Transfer to a serving dish and set aside at room temperature.

9. Heat the remaining 2 tablespoons canola oil in a large sauté pan over medium-high heat. Season the tuna with remaining ½ teaspoon salt and sear for 30–45 seconds on each side. With a sharp knife, slice the rare-in-the-center tuna into ½-inch-thick pieces.

10. Lay tuna atop the eggplant caponata, season with sea salt, and serve.

Italian Fish Tacos with Fennel Slaw and Basil Aioli

I love tacos, and fish tacos are one of my favorite things to make. Fennel slaw and basil aioli give these fish tacos a Mediterranean feel. Flour tortillas are preferable to corn for the tacos in this recipe because they are softer and more pliable. If you can't find bluefish for this recipe, you could use tilapia or striped bass.

1. Heat an indoor grill pan or an outdoor grill to medium-high. In a medium saucepan, bring the water, champagne vinegar, and sugar to a boil over high heat, stirring to dissolve the sugar.

2. Combine the fennel, onion, pepper, and carrot in a large heatproof mixing bowl. When the liquid comes to a boil, remove from heat and pour it over the vegetables. Let the vegetables marinate at room temperature until cooled, about 15–20 minutes. Strain and discard the liquid. Toss olive oil, fennel fronds, and ¼ teaspoon salt with the vegetables.

3. Evenly brush the bluefish filets on all sides with canola oil and season with remaining ½ teaspoon salt. Grill the bluefish for 2–3 minutes on each side, or until just cooked. While the fish is cooking, warm the tortillas on the grill.

4. To assemble, spoon *Basil Aioli* into the tortillas and top with bluefish and fennel slaw. Serve immediately.

SERVES 4 PEOPLE AS A SMALL PLATE; MAKES 8 SMALL TACOS
ACTIVE TIME = 30 MINUTES
INACTIVE TIME = 20 MINUTES

———————★———————

1 cup water

½ cup champagne vinegar

½ cup sugar

½ cup shaved fennel bulb

¼ cup thinly sliced red onion

¼ cup thinly sliced red bell pepper, seeds and ribs removed

¼ cup shredded carrot

1 tablespoon extra virgin olive oil

2 teaspoons fennel fronds

¼ teaspoon plus ½ teaspoon kosher salt

¾-pound cleaned bluefish filet, skin removed, cut into 8 equal pieces (1.5 ounces each)

1 tablespoon canola oil

8 small (5-inch) flour tortillas

½ cup *Basil Aioli* (recipe follows)

Basil Aioli

1. Bring a medium saucepan of water to a boil. Set a bowl of ice water to the side. Blanch the basil leaves for 30 seconds and shock in ice water. Squeeze all the water from the leaves and rough chop.

2. In a food processor or blender, blend the basil, garlic, egg yolks, lemon juice, and salt for 10 seconds on medium speed.

3. With the food processor on, slowly add the canola oil. Blend for 15 seconds, or until a thick emulsion forms.

MAKES APPROXIMATELY ¾ CUP
ACTIVE TIME = 15 MINUTES

————★————

16 large basil leaves

2 cloves *Roasted Garlic* (page 62)

2 large egg yolks

1 tablespoon lemon juice

½ teaspoon kosher salt

½ cup canola oil

————★————

THE AIOLI IS BEST CONSUMED THE SAME DAY IT'S MADE. IT WILL TURN BROWN IF REFRIGERATED LONGER THAN 8 HOURS.

————★————

USE A MANDOLINE TO SLICE THE VEGETABLES AS THIN AS YOU CAN.

Slow-Roasted Bass with Stewed Artichokes, Pine Nuts, and Bacon

SERVES 4 AS A SMALL PLATE

ACTIVE TIME = 1 HOUR

———————★———————

1 lemon, quartered

5 large artichokes

3 tablespoons extra virgin olive oil

1 cup ¼-inch diced thick-cut bacon (approximately 2 slices)

½ cup small-diced shallot

½ cup baby carrots; peeled, greens removed, and thinly sliced into discs

2 cloves garlic, thinly sliced

1 teaspoon plus ¼ teaspoon kosher salt

1 cup white wine

2 sprigs thyme

1 bay leaf

1 cup chicken broth or stock

1 pound striped bass filet; skin removed, cut into 4 equal portions

¼ cup pine nuts

1 tablespoon finely chopped parsley

I like to use Sauvignon Blanc or Pinot Grigio in this dish because both wines are crisp, with a great acidity that complements the bass. If you can't find striped bass, try this recipe with halibut, cod, or black sea bass.

1. Preheat the oven to 300°F.

2. Fill a large mixing bowl with cold water. Squeeze the lemon into the water, then drop the lemon quarters in.

3. To clean the artichokes, cut off and discard all but 1 inch of the stem. Remove all outer leaves until you only see soft yellow and purple leaves. Grab the top center purplish leaves and pull them apart to reveal the fuzzy center. Scoop out and discard all of the fuzz. With a paring knife, remove the outer green part of the stem until you see mostly white flesh. Slice each artichoke heart into 6 pieces and store in the lemon water until ready to cook.

4. Heat the olive oil in a large sauté pan over medium heat. Add the bacon and sauté for 8–10 minutes or until just crispy. Pour out and reserve 1 tablespoon of rendered bacon fat for later use.

5. Add the shallot to the pan with the bacon and sweat for approximately 2–3 minutes or until soft and translucent. Drain the artichokes, pat dry with paper towels

or a clean dishtowel, and add to the pan. Toss in the carrots, garlic, and 1 teaspoon salt. Sauté for 2 minutes, until the garlic becomes fragrant.

6. Add the white wine, thyme, and bay leaf to the pan, and bring to a high simmer for about 5–10 minutes to reduce liquid by half. Add chicken stock, bring to a boil, then lower heat and simmer for 15 minutes, or until the artichoke hearts are fork-tender.

7. Brush the fish with reserved bacon fat and season with remaining ¼ teaspoon salt. Roast in the oven on a baking sheet for 16–18 minutes. The bass is done when a cake tester slides out easily with no resistance and the end is warm to the touch.

8. Toast pine nuts in a dry sauté pan over medium heat for 5 minutes, shaking the pan often to prevent burning. Add the pine nuts to the artichoke mixture. Remove thyme and bay leaf. Stir in the parsley and bring to a simmer.

9. Transfer the artichoke stew to a serving dish, top with bass, and serve.

Grilled Whole Bass with Warm Tomato Vinaigrette

This is a great summertime family-style dish where everyone will want to just dig in and eat the fish right off the serving platter. Grilling whole bass is really easy—just have the guy at the fish counter at your grocery store or fish market scale and gut the fish for you.

1. Preheat an outdoor grill to medium-high heat.

2. Rinse the fish under cold, running water and pat dry with paper towels or a clean dishtowel. Brush each bass inside and out with 2 tablespoons olive oil and season with 2 teaspoons salt.

3. Place the fish in a nonstick fish-grilling basket, or use bunched-up paper towels to apply canola oil to the grill grate to prevent sticking, if you want to put the fish directly on the grill.

4. Grill the bass over direct heat for 8–10 minutes on each side. The skin will become crispy and the flesh cooked through. Keep the grill cover closed while the fish is cooking.

5. Heat the remaining ¼ cup olive oil in a large sauté pan over medium heat. Sweat the shallots for 2 minutes until soft and translucent. Toss in the tomatoes and sauté for 2 minutes. Stir in the jalapeño and sauté for 1 minute. Remove from heat and stir in lemon juice and remaining 1 teaspoon salt.

6. Transfer the grilled bass to a serving platter and top with warm tomato vinaigrette.

SERVES 4, FAMILY STYLE, AS A MAIN COURSE
ACTIVE TIME = 30 MINUTES

———— ★ ————

2 whole bass (1¼ pounds each), gutted and scales removed

2 tablespoons plus ¼ cup extra virgin olive oil

2 teaspoons plus 1 teaspoon kosher salt

¼ cup thinly sliced shallot

2 cups quartered grape tomatoes (yellow, red, and orange)

2 teaspoons finely minced jalapeño

1½ tablespoons lemon juice

SERVES 4 AS A SMALL PLATE

ACTIVE TIME = 55–60 MINUTES

———————— ★ ————————

3 ears fresh corn; shucked, brushed lightly with olive oil, and seasoned with salt

1 tablespoon extra virgin olive oil

1 tablespoon unsalted butter

3 cups chanterelle mushrooms (about ⅔ pound)

½ teaspoon plus ¼ teaspoon kosher salt

¼ cup small-diced shallot

½ teaspoon thyme leaves

¼ cup thinly sliced scallion (green part only)

3 tablespoons canola oil

1-pound striped bass filet, skin removed, cut into 4 equal portions

4 tablespoons *Parsley Butter*, cut into 4 even discs (recipe follows)

Striped Bass with Grilled Corn, Chanterelle, and Parsley Butter

I like making herb butters. Whether you spread them on toast or melt them over fish or other meats, they just add such a nice freshness and flavor to almost any dish. The parsley butter in this dish brings a nice Italian finish to the fish, corn, and chanterelle mushrooms.

1. Preheat outdoor grill or indoor grill pan to medium-high. Grill corn for 2–3 minutes on all sides. When corn has cooled enough to handle, cut the kernels from the cob and set aside.

2. Heat olive oil and butter in a large sauté pan over medium heat and sauté chanterelles for 1 minute. Season with ½ teaspoon salt and sauté for 4–5 minutes, or until soft and tender.

3. Add shallot and sauté for 2 minutes. Stir in grilled corn, thyme leaves, and scallion and reduce heat to medium-low to keep warm.

4. Heat canola oil in a separate large sauté pan over high heat. Season the striped bass filets with the remaining ¼ teaspoon salt, then add them to the pan, searing for 3 minutes on each side.

5. Transfer corn mixture to a serving dish and top with seared bass. Top each piece of fish with a disc of *Parsley Butter*, which will melt over the fish and act as a sauce. Serve immediately.

Parsley Butter

1. Combine all ingredients in a mixing bowl and whisk with a fork to incorporate.

2. Transfer to a sheet of plastic wrap and roll into a 3-inch-long cylinder.

3. Twist the ends of the plastic wrap, and tie each end in a knot to hold the butter in a cylindrical shape.

4. Refrigerate for an hour, or until solid.

MAKES 4 TABLESPOONS
ACTIVE TIME = 5 MINUTES
INACTIVE TIME = 1 HOUR

———★———

PARSLEY BUTTER

4 tablespoons unsalted butter, room temperature

1 tablespoon finely chopped flat-leaf parsley

¼ teaspoon kosher salt

⅛ teaspoon ground red chili flakes

1 teaspoon lemon zest

———★———

BUTTER CAN BE REFRIGERATED FOR 2 WEEKS OR FROZEN FOR 3 MONTHS.

Tuna Carpaccio

ACTIVE TIME = 35–40 MINUTES

———★———

2 teaspoons coriander seeds

1 teaspoon black peppercorns

½ teaspoon fennel seeds

1 cup water

¾ cup white wine (Chardonnay recommended)

Peel of ½ lemon (no pith) plus
1 tablespoon juice

Peel of ½ orange (no pith) plus
1 tablespoon juice

¼ cup thinly sliced shallot

¼ cup small-diced celery

⅛ ounce dried porcini mushrooms

2 teaspoons minced ginger

¼ teaspoon kosher salt

(INGREDIENTS CONTINUE NEXT PAGE)

This is a clean, light, and fragrant dish with just enough heat to keep it interesting. The ginger and citrus not only enhance the flavor of the tuna, they open up your palate, allowing you to taste the big flavors in the broth.

1. Toast the coriander, peppercorns, and fennel seeds in a dry sauté pan over medium heat for 5 minutes, shaking the pan often to prevent burning.

2. In a medium saucepan, bring the water, wine, lemon and orange peel, shallot, celery, porcini mushrooms, ginger, salt, chili flakes, basil stems, mint stem, and toasted spices to a boil over high heat. Lower the heat and simmer for 15 minutes. Cover, remove from heat, and let steep for 15 minutes.

3. Place the tuna between two sheets of plastic wrap. Using a flat mallet, very gently pound the slices to ⅛ inch thick. Lay the tuna in a single layer in a large, shallow serving bowl or dish. Cover with plastic wrap and refrigerate.

4. In a small mixing bowl, toss the radish, cucumber, basil, and olive oil.

5. Strain the steeped ginger-mushroom broth into a mixing bowl and discard the solids. Stir in the lemon and orange juices.

6. Remove the tuna from the refrigerator and spoon just enough broth over it to cover it. Garnish with the radish-cucumber salad and serve.

⅛ teaspoon red chili flakes

3 basil stems without leaves

1 mint stem with leaves

¾ pound sushi-grade tuna loin, sliced into ¼-inch-thick pieces

¼ cup small-diced radish

¼ cup small-diced English cucumber

1 tablespoon finely chopped basil

2 teaspoons extra virgin olive oil

¼ teaspoon sea salt (Maldon recommended)

———————— ★ ————————

USE A VEGETABLE PEELER TO GET
THE CITRUS PEEL WITHOUT ANY OF
THE WHITE, BITTER PITH.

Whole Roasted Fluke with Lemon, Capers, and Dill

You can prepare the fluke for roasting according to the instructions below, or you can have the person at the fish counter do it for you. If you can't find fluke, flounder or sole would work, as well. This fish preparation is super-easy, and the capers and dill really give this great flavor.

1. Preheat the oven to 450°F. Using a sharp knife, remove the head and fins from the fluke. With the fluke lying flat on its side, make a cut just above the tail and along the back. Pull back and discard the skin, exposing the top filets. Flip over and repeat with the other side, exposing the filets. Keep the filets on the bone.

2. Heat the canola oil in a large, oven-safe sauté pan over high heat.

3. In a bowl, whisk the flour and 1 teaspoon salt together. Evenly dust the fish with this mixture.

4. Lay the fluke flat in the hot oil for 3 minutes, or until golden brown. Turn the fish over, and place the sauté pan in the oven. Roast for 10–12 minutes or until the fish is just cooked through.

5. In a small bowl, whisk the olive oil into the lemon juice to make a vinaigrette. Whisk in the capers, dill, and remaining ¼ teaspoon salt.

6. Transfer the fish to a large serving dish and pour the vinaigrette over it. Serve whole.

SERVES 4 AS A SMALL PLATE

ACTIVE TIME = 25–30 MINUTES

———————★———————

1 whole fluke (2 pounds) gutted

2 tablespoons canola oil

2 teaspoons all-purpose flour

1¼ teaspoons kosher salt

¼ cup extra virgin olive oil

3 tablespoons fresh lemon juice

1 tablespoon capers, finely chopped

1 teaspoon chopped dill

Yellowfin Tuna Crudo with Crushed Pine Nuts and Aged Balsamic

SERVES 4 AS A SMALL PLATE

ACTIVE TIME = 40 MINUTES

———— ★ ————

½ cup small-diced shallot

½ cup extra virgin olive oil

¼ cup pine nuts

Zest of ½ lemon

10 mint leaves, finely chopped

¾ pound sushi-grade yellowfin tuna loin, sliced into ¼-inch-thick pieces

¼ teaspoon sea salt (Maldon recommended)

10 whole mint leaves, torn

2 teaspoons aged balsamic vinegar (25 years, preferred)

———— ★ ————

YOU CAN MAKE THE SHALLOT OIL IN STEP 1 A DAY IN ADVANCE AND STORE, COVERED, AT ROOM TEMPERATURE.

It's worth spending a little more to buy good aged balsamic vinegar for this recipe. Balsamic vinegar is pungent and sweet and brings out the natural tuna flavor in this dish.

1. In a small saucepan, bring the shallot and olive oil to a simmer over medium heat. Reduce the heat to low and simmer for 30 minutes until the shallots are very soft. Remove from heat to let cool at room temperature.

2. Toast the pine nuts in a dry sauté pan over medium heat for 5 minutes, shaking the pan often to prevent burning. Remove from heat, place the pine nuts on a cutting board, and gently crush them with the bottom of a heavy saucepan or Dutch oven.

3. Add the crushed pine nuts, lemon zest, and chopped mint leaves to the shallot and olive oil.

4. Arrange the tuna on a serving platter and pour the shallot mixture over it. Season with sea salt and garnish with torn mint leaves. Finish with a drizzle of aged balsamic vinegar.

10 gone hogging

A COUPLE YEARS AGO, I was asked to help roast four pigs. But not in someone's backyard for a barbecue. No, this was roasting four pigs, each in its own *caja china*, on the rooftop of the Marriott Marquis hotel in New York for the James Beard Awards.

We cut our timing really close—so close that we ended up having to wheel the pigs into the hotel ballroom during the reception, ashes flying everywhere, saying, "Excuse me, please!" to people in tuxedos and fancy dresses. I remember pushing one of the roasting boxes into the room and seeing Eric Ripert, Jean-Georges Vongerichten, Michelle Bernstein, Aarón Sanchez—all heroes of mine. It was already special to be asked to cook for people you admire. But to actually get to see them? It was a night I'll never forget.

I've since come to know some of my chef heroes as friends, and one of the many things we have in common is that we love roasting pigs. It's amazing what something as simple as heat can do. It probably won't surprise you that I'm a fan of all parts of the pig: the ribs, belly, loin, chops, shoulder. I like it roasted, fried, braised, cured—you name it, I'll eat it. Hope you will, too. And for the ambitious, I've included a recipe in this chapter that I hope will encourage you to roast a whole pig and share it with friends and family.

Crispy Bacon with Poached Egg and Mustard Aioli

SERVES 4 AS A SMALL PLATE

ACTIVE TIME = 1 HOUR

INACTIVE TIME = 1 HOUR, 30 MINUTES

———— ★ ————

1 tablespoon plus 6 cups (for deep frying) canola oil

½ pound slab bacon

½ cup small-diced onion

1 garlic clove, thinly sliced

1 tablespoon Dijon mustard

2 sprigs thyme

1 bay leaf

1 quart chicken broth

¼ cup all-purpose flour

1 large egg, beaten, plus 4 fresh large eggs, whole, for poaching

½ cup panko bread crumbs

1 tablespoon white vinegar

½ cup *Mustard Aioli* (recipe follows)

Sea salt, to taste

1 tablespoon finely chopped chives

Buy the freshest eggs you can find to poach for this dish. The fresher they are, the more cleanly they poach. When the runny yolk mixes with the Mustard Aioli and bacon, it's just so silky and creamy and perfect.

1. Preheat oven to 350°F.

2. Heat 1 tablespoon canola oil in a large, heavy-bottomed pot over medium-high heat. Score the top of the slab bacon ⅛ inch deep and ¾ inch apart.

3. Sear the bacon slab in the hot oil, scored side down, for 3 minutes on both sides, or until golden brown and crispy. Remove bacon from the pot and set aside.

4. Reduce heat to medium, and sweat the onions for 2–3 minutes, or until soft and translucent. Add garlic and sauté for 2 minutes.

5. Stir in mustard, thyme, and bay leaf. Add chicken broth and bring to a slight boil.

6. Return seared bacon to pot, cover with lid, and braise in the oven for 1 hour. The bacon will become soft and plump.

7. Remove from the oven and let bacon cool in the liquid for 10 minutes. Lower oven temperature to 300°F.

8. Remove bacon from the liquid and refrigerate the bacon for 20 minutes. When cooled, slice into four

equal pieces. Pat dry with a paper towel to remove any excess moisture.

9. Heat 6 cups of canola oil in an electric deep fryer to 350°F. If you do not have an electric fryer, use a heavy-bottomed pot and a candy thermometer.

10. Set up the breading station with three separate shallow bowls for flour, beaten egg, and bread crumbs.

11. Dredge each bacon slice in the flour, then egg, then the bread crumbs. Patting the bread crumbs on the bacon will ensure they stick.

12. Gently drop each piece of breaded bacon into the oil and fry for 3–4 minutes or until the breading is crispy and golden brown. Remove from fryer and drain on paper towels. Transfer to a baking sheet and keep warm in the oven until ready to serve.

13. To poach the eggs, bring a medium saucepan of water to a simmer (around 185°F) and add vinegar. Vinegar helps keep the egg together while it's poaching and helps the white of the egg encase the yolk.

14. Crack each egg into a small dish to have more control of the egg as you release it into the water to poach. Before adding the egg to the pan, stir the water in one direction to create a whirlpool, then gently slide the egg into the water. The whirlpool will hold the egg together and allow the white to encase the yolk. Repeat with a second egg and let them poach for 2–2½ minutes until the whites are cooked and the yolks are warm and runny.

15. Carefully lift the eggs out of the water with a slotted spoon, and pat the bottom of the spoon with a paper towel to remove any excess water. Set aside on a plate.

16. Repeat step 14 with the remaining 2 eggs and set aside with the first 2 poached eggs.

17. Evenly spread *Mustard Aioli* on four small plates. Place a piece of bacon on top of the aioli slightly off center and add a poached egg to the side. Season with sea salt and garnish with chives. Serve immediately.

Mustard Aioli

1. Blend roasted garlic, egg yolk, lemon juice, whole-grain mustard, Dijon mustard, Worcestershire sauce, Tabasco sauce, and salt in a blender for 15 seconds on medium speed.

2. With blender running, slowly add canola oil and blend for 15–20 seconds, until a thick emulsion forms.

MAKES APPROXIMATELY ⅔ CUP
ACTIVE TIME = 10 MINUTES

———————★———————

MUSTARD AIOLI

2 cloves *Roasted Garlic* (page 62)

1 large egg yolk

1 tablespoon lemon juice

2 teaspoons whole-grain mustard

1½ teaspoons Dijon mustard

½ teaspoon Worcestershire sauce

¼ teaspoon Tabasco sauce

¼ teaspoon kosher salt

½ cup canola oil

———————★———————

THE AIOLI CAN BE REFRIGERATED FOR UP TO 5 DAYS.

Pork Belly with White Beans and Country Ham

SERVES 4 AS A SMALL PLATE

ACTIVE TIME = 45 MINUTES

INACTIVE TIME = 3 HOURS

———————★———————

2 tablespoons canola oil

1¼ pounds pork belly, skin removed

1 cup small-diced onion

½ cup small-diced celery

½ cup small-diced carrot

1 tablespoon minced garlic

1 quart chicken broth

¼ cup plus 1 tablespoon lard

¼ cup finely chopped country ham

1 (15-ounce) can white beans, drained and rinsed

½ teaspoon kosher salt

This is pork and beans like you've never had it before. You start with a cured piece of pork belly and plump it by braising it, so it becomes unctuous and fatty. Mashed white beans and country ham pull it all together.

1. Preheat the oven to 325°F.

2. Heat the canola oil in a large, heavy-bottomed pot (oven-safe) or Dutch oven over medium-high heat. Sear the pork belly for 3 minutes on each side. Remove from pot and set aside.

3. Reduce the heat to medium and add the onions, celery, carrot, and garlic. Sweat for 3–4 minutes or until soft and translucent.

4. Add the chicken broth and bring to a slight boil. Return the pork belly to the pot, cover, and braise in the oven for 2½–3 hours. Check it after 2 hours and every 30 minutes after to test for tenderness. Remove from oven when pork belly is tender and succulent. Let the pork belly cool for 20 minutes in the liquid.

5. Heat ¼ cup lard in a large sauté pan over medium-high heat. When the lard has melted and is bubbling, add the country ham and sauté for 4 minutes. Reduce heat to medium and add the beans and salt. Sauté for 10 minutes until soft and tender. The beans will begin

to break down and incorporate with the lard. Stir until a chunky purée forms. Remove from heat and let rest at room temperature.

6. Remove the pork belly from the braising liquid, and discard the liquid.

7. Slice the pork belly into four equal portions. Heat the remaining 1 tablespoon lard in a large sauté pan. When the lard has melted and is bubbling, sear the pork belly for 3 minutes each on top and bottom until golden brown and crispy.

8. Reheat the beans and spread on a large serving dish. Arrange the pork belly on top and serve.

Pig in a Box with Sour Orange Relish

SERVES A MINIMUM OF 10 PEOPLE

ACTIVE TIME = 4 HOURS

INACTIVE TIME = 12 HOURS

————————— ★ —————————

PIG

2 gallons plus 2 gallons water

8 cups kosher salt

2 cups light brown sugar

30-pound suckling pig, precut by your butcher or meat purveyor for easy butterflying

30 pounds charcoal briquettes (Kingsford recommended)

(INGREDIENTS CONTINUE NEXT PAGE)

————————— ★ —————————

SEE ROASTING SEQUENCE ON FOLLOWING SPREAD

Everybody should roast a whole pig at least once in their lives. To do this recipe, you'll need a metal-lined pig-roasting box (with a roasting rack inside)—often called a caja china *or a* caja asadora. *You might be able to find one at a specialty outdoor goods store, but I ordered mine online (they're really easy to put together!). This is a fun recipe to make when you're having a big party. Your friends can help with the actual roasting, and it's a great outdoor cookout activity.*

1. Bring 2 gallons water, salt, and sugar to a boil, stirring until salt and sugar dissolve. Refrigerate, or place stockpot in an ice-filled sink to chill the brine.

2. Place pig in a large plastic container and add the chilled brine and remaining 2 gallons of water. Cover and refrigerate for 12 hours.

3. Remove pig from the brine and pat dry with paper towels or a clean dishtowel.

4. Press down on the pig's chest to crack the bones, allowing the pig to be splayed open and lay flat. Lock butterflied pig into the roasting rack belly up, place rack in box, and close the lid. Pour 10 pounds of charcoal onto the lid, and light.

5. Roast for 1 hour, then add 10 more pounds of charcoal.

6. Roast for another hour, then carefully remove lid with coals. Open the box and flip the pig onto its belly. Replace the lid and add remaining 10 pounds of charcoal. Roast for 1 more hour, for a total of 3 hours.

7. While pig is roasting, toast cumin seeds in a dry sauté pan over medium heat for 5 minutes, shaking pan often to prevent burning. Transfer to a spice grinder and grind into a powder. Put powder into a large mixing bowl.

8. Supreme eight of the oranges (page 39) and place the segments in the mixing bowl. Squeeze out any of the remaining orange juice into the bowl. Juice the remaining two oranges into the bowl.

9. Add remaining ingredients for the relish to the bowl and stir to combine. Refrigerate up to 2 hours.

10. Remove pig from the roasting box and transfer to a large cutting board. Break it down into large pieces and transfer to a large serving platter. Pour the sour orange relish over the pork, and serve.

SOUR ORANGE RELISH

1 tablespoon cumin seeds

10 navel oranges

1½ cups extra virgin olive oil

½ cup small-diced red onion

½ cup thinly sliced scallions, green part only

½ cup finely chopped parsley

¼ cup lime juice

2 tablespoons dried oregano

1 tablespoon minced garlic

1 tablespoon sugar

1 teaspoon kosher salt

———————★———————

IF YOU DON'T HAVE A LARGE ENOUGH CONTAINER OR ROOM IN YOUR FRIDGE, YOU CAN BRINE THE PIG IN A CLEAN GARBAGE BAG AND KEEP IT COLD IN A BATHTUB FILLED WITH ICE. YOU'LL NEED TO REPLENISH THE ICE A FEW TIMES OVER THE 12-HOUR BRINING PROCESS TO KEEP THE TEMPERATURE BETWEEN 32–40°F.

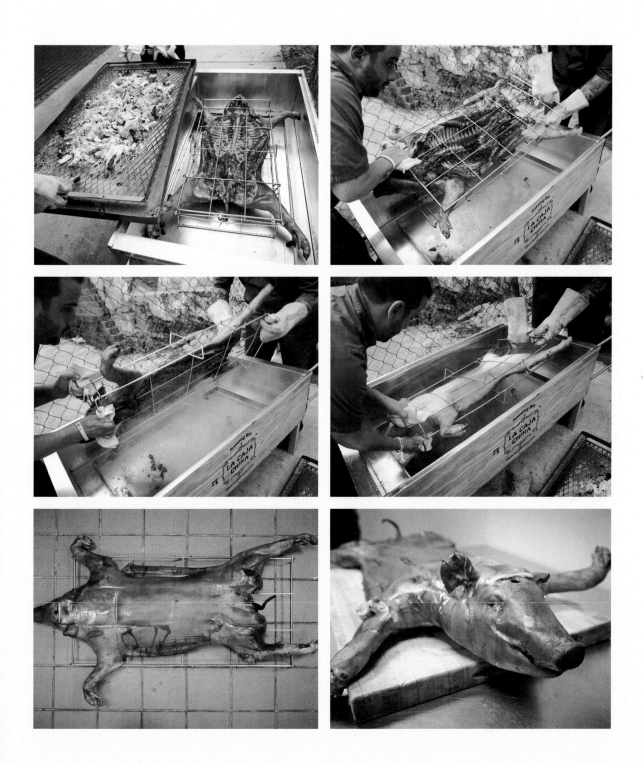

Pork Shoulder Braised in Spicy Tomato Broth with Clams, Corn, and Potato

SERVES 4–6 AS A SMALL PLATE

ACTIVE TIME = 30–35 MINUTES

INACTIVE TIME = 1 HOUR, 55 MINUTES

———————★———————

3 tablespoons canola oil

¾ pound boneless pork shoulder; cut into 1-inch cubes

1 teaspoon kosher salt

1 cup small-diced onion

½ cup small-diced red bell pepper

1 tablespoon minced garlic

2 tablespoons tomato paste

2 teaspoons red chili flakes

3 cups chicken broth

1 cup canned crushed tomatoes

1 bay leaf

½ pound baby golden potatoes, cut into ½-inch cubes

(INGREDIENTS CONTINUE NEXT PAGE)

This feels like a perfect dish for late summer into early fall—when the evenings are cool, and you want dinner with a little more oomph to it. Braised pork shoulder is easy to make, and the clams, corn, and potato make this a really nice one-pot meal. The garlic and chili flakes add just enough heat to this dish to make it really interesting, but not blow your head off.

1. Preheat oven to 350°F.

2. Heat canola oil in a large, heavy-bottomed pot over medium-high heat. Season pork with salt.

3. When the oil is hot and shimmering, sear the pork in batches for 2 minutes on each side or until golden brown. Remove pork and set aside.

4. Lower heat to medium, and sweat the onions for 2–3 minutes, or until soft and translucent. Add bell pepper and garlic, and sweat them for another 2 minutes.

5. Add tomato paste and red chili flakes, and cook for 2–3 minutes, stirring occasionally. Stir in chicken broth, crushed tomatoes, and bay leaf, and bring to a low boil. Return seared pork to the pot, cover, and braise in the oven for 1 hour.

6. Remove from the oven and add the potatoes and corn kernels. Cover and return to the oven for another 45 minutes.

7. Remove from the oven and add the clams. Cover and return to the oven for an additional 10 minutes or until the clams have opened. Discard any clams that didn't open.

8. Remove from the oven and stir in the parsley. Transfer to a large serving dish or individual serving bowls. Serve immediately with the lemon wedges on the side.

Kernels from 2 ears of corn

12 littleneck clams, cleaned

1 tablespoon finely chopped parsley

1 lemon, quartered

Roasted Ribs with Oregano and Coriander Yogurt

SERVES 4 AS A SMALL PLATE

ACTIVE TIME = 45–50 MINUTES

INACTIVE TIME = 2 HOURS, 30 MINUTES

———————★———————

¼ cup coriander seeds

¼ cup dried oregano

1 rack baby back ribs, cut into 3-bone pieces

½ teaspoon plus ½ teaspoon kosher salt

¼ cup canola oil

1 cup medium-diced onion

¼ cup thinly sliced garlic

4 sprigs thyme

1 bay leaf

1½ quarts chicken broth

1 lemon, quartered

½ teaspoon sea salt (Maldon recommended)

1 cup *Coriander Yogurt* (recipe follows)

The coriander-oregano rub is the trick to making these ribs so flavorful. Serving them with coriander yogurt augments the pork's natural flavor. If you like, you could garnish the ribs with sliced radish, orange, and fresh parsley for added crunch.

1. Preheat the oven to 350°F.

2. Toast the coriander seeds in a dry sauté pan over medium heat for 5 minutes, shaking pan often to prevent burning. Transfer the seeds to a spice grinder and grind into a powder. Mix with dried oregano and divide into two equal portions.

3. Season ribs with one portion of the coriander/oregano powder and ½ teaspoon salt.

4. Heat canola oil in a large, heavy-bottomed pot (oven-safe) or Dutch oven over medium-high heat and sear the ribs for 2–3 minutes, or until golden brown. Because the ribs are curved, use the outer edges of the pot to get a good sear. You will have to sear in batches depending on the size of your pot. Let the seared ribs rest on a cutting board at room temperature.

5. In the same pot, sweat the onions for 2–3 minutes over medium heat or until soft and translucent. If they start to brown, add a teaspoon of water to slow the cooking process.

6. Add the garlic and sauté for 1 minute.

7. Stir in the thyme, bay leaf, seared ribs, and chicken broth. Increase the heat to bring to a low boil, cover, and braise in the oven for 2 hours or until the meat is tender and pulls clean away from the bone.

8. Remove from the oven and let the ribs cool in the liquid for 30 minutes. Increase the oven temperature to 375°F.

9. Take the ribs out of the liquid and transfer them to a baking sheet, meat side up. Season with remaining coriander/oregano powder and ½ teaspoon salt. Roast in the oven for 6–8 minutes or until a golden brown crust forms.

10. Stack the ribs on large serving platter. Squeeze lemon over the ribs and season with sea salt. Serve immediately with the *Coriander Yogurt* on the side.

Coriander Yogurt

1. Toast the coriander seeds in a dry sauté pan over medium heat for 5 minutes, shaking the pan often to prevent burning. Transfer the seeds to a spice grinder and grind into a powder.

2. Combine the ground coriander with the remaining ingredients in a small mixing bowl. Stir, cover, and let rest at room temperature for 30 minutes. Refrigerate until you are ready to use.

3. Bring to room temperature at least 30 minutes before serving.

MAKES APPROXIMATELY 1 CUP
ACTIVE TIME = 10–15 MINUTES
INACTIVE TIME = 30 MINUTES

———— ★ ————

CORIANDER YOGURT

1 tablespoon coriander seeds

1 cup plain Greek yogurt

1 teaspoon orange zest

1 teaspoon lemon juice

1 teaspoon extra virgin olive oil

½ teaspoon kosher salt

———— ★ ————

YOGURT CAN BE REFRIGERATED FOR 3 DAYS.

Salt-Roasted Pork Tenderloin with Prosciutto and Charred Ramp Pesto

SERVES 4 AS A SMALL PLATE

ACTIVE TIME = 50–60 MINUTES

———————★———————

4 large egg whites

2 tablespoons minced garlic

2 tablespoons water

4 cups kosher salt

2 tablespoons canola oil

1-pound pork tenderloin, silver skin removed

½ cup *Charred Ramp Pesto* (recipe follows)

I love salt-roasted food. Encasing meat in a salt crust helps the meat steam itself, because the salt keeps all the moisture locked in there, giving you the most tender, flavorful end result. When I'm feeling creative, I'll shape the salt mixture around the piece of pork I'm roasting into the shape of a pig. Or, if I'm roasting fish, I'll shape the salt to look like a fish. It's very old-school restaurant-style to then take it tableside, crack open the crust, and slice the meat right there.

1. Preheat the oven to 375°F.

2. Whisk the egg whites in a large mixing bowl for 3–4 minutes or until they form soft peaks. Add the garlic, water, and salt and stir until it resembles shaved ice.

3. Heat the canola oil in a large sauté pan over medium-high heat. Sear the pork on all sides until golden brown, approximately 8–10 minutes.

4. Line a baking sheet with parchment paper. Scoop 1 cup of the salt mixture onto the sheet and flatten it into the size and shape of the tenderloin. Place the seared tenderloin on top and cover with the remaining salt mixture. Press down and around to make sure the salt is tightly packed and the pork fully covered. Carefully

insert a meat thermometer, making sure the salt pack stays intact.

5. Roast for 20 minutes or until the pork's internal temperature reads 140°F. Remove from the oven and let rest for 5 minutes. Gently remove the thermometer.

6. Use the back of a spoon to crack the salt crust and break it away, exposing the tenderloin. Transfer the pork to a cutting board and use a pastry brush to remove any excess salt. Slice the tenderloin on the bias into ½-inch pieces and place on a large serving platter. Spoon ¼ cup of *Charred Ramp Pesto* over the pork and serve immediately with the remaining pesto on the side.

Charred Ramp Pesto

1. Toast the walnuts in a dry sauté pan over medium heat for 5 minutes, shaking the pan often to prevent burning.

2. Heat an indoor grill pan or outdoor grill to high heat. If you recently rinsed the ramp leaves, pat them dry with paper towels. Grill on each side for 20–30 seconds until slightly wilted and charred.

3. In a food processor, combine the walnuts, charred ramp leaves, pickled ramp stems, and salt. Turn on the processor and slowly add in the olive oil until a paste forms, approximately 30 seconds.

MAKES APPROXIMATELY ½ CUP
ACTIVE TIME = 20–25 MINUTES

————— ★ —————

CHARRED RAMP PESTO

2 tablespoons raw walnuts

2 cups whole ramp leaves, tightly packed

6 *Pickled Ramps* (page 58)

½ teaspoon kosher salt

⅓ cup extra virgin olive oil

————— ★ —————

PESTO CAN BE REFRIGERATED FOR UP TO 3 DAYS.

Pork Chop with Roasted Butternut Squash and Red Wine Onions

SERVES 4 AS A SMALL PLATE

ACTIVE TIME = 1 HOUR, 10 MINUTES

——————★——————

BUTTERNUT SQUASH

1 small butternut squash
(1¼–1½ pounds)

1 tablespoon extra virgin olive oil

½ teaspoon kosher salt

2 tablespoons plus 1 tablespoon
unsalted butter

2 sprigs rosemary

RED WINE ONIONS

1 cup red pearl onions, peeled

1 cup red wine

½ cup red wine vinegar

1 tablespoon sugar

(INGREDIENTS CONTINUE NEXT PAGE)

I like red onions because they're a little more pungent and stand out more in a dish. Glazing them in red wine mellows them a little, but their acidity complements the salty pork and the sweet squash. Big flavors all around.

1. Preheat the oven to 375°F.

2. Cut the butternut squash in half lengthwise and scoop out and discard the seeds. Lay the squash flesh side up on a baking sheet. Drizzle with olive oil and season with salt. Place 1 tablespoon of butter and 1 rosemary sprig in each half where the seeds were removed. Cover the squash tightly with aluminum foil and roast for 45 minutes or until tender.

3. While the squash is roasting, heat the pearl onions, red wine, red wine vinegar, and sugar in a medium saucepan and bring to a boil. Reduce the heat and simmer for 30 minutes, or until the liquid becomes a thick syrup. Remove from the heat and let rest at room temperature.

4. Take out the squash, uncover it, and remove and discard rosemary sprigs. Keep the oven on. When the squash has cooled enough to handle, scoop out the flesh and sauté it with 1 tablespoon butter in a large sauté pan over medium-high heat for 5–7 minutes, until

PORK CHOPS

2 tablespoons canola oil

2 (8-ounce) boneless pork chops

½ teaspoon kosher salt

¼ teaspoon freshly cracked black pepper

¼ teaspoon sea salt (Maldon recommended)

the squash becomes golden brown. Remove from heat and set aside at room temperature.

5. Heat the canola oil in a large oven-safe sauté pan over medium-high heat. Season the pork chops with salt and pepper and sear for 5–7 minutes on each side, or until golden brown and cooked to an internal temperature of 140°F. Remove the chops and let rest for 5 minutes at room temperature.

6. Reheat the onions and butternut squash in their respective pans over medium heat. Slice the pork into ¼-inch slices. Spoon the caramelized butternut squash onto a serving dish. Place sliced pork on top and spoon red wine onions over the pork. Season with sea salt and serve.

Sausage and Peppers

As a lifelong Yankees fan, making sausage and peppers "Fenway Style" is a tough call, but well worth it. You just shave the heck out of red and yellow bell peppers and onions, and they cook more evenly and are easier to eat. I add a little ketchup to the peppers when I make them because it's a nice binder, and it reminds me of the baseball games and street festivals where I first had sausage and peppers.

1. Heat the canola oil in a large sauté pan over medium-high heat. Sear the sausage for 2 minutes on all sides, until golden brown. Remove from pan and set aside.

2. Lower the heat to medium and sweat the onions for 3–4 minutes, until soft and translucent. Stir in red and yellow bell peppers and salt, and sauté for 5–6 minutes or until peppers are soft.

3. Return the sausage to the pan. Add the bay leaf, water, and ketchup. Sauté over medium heat, stirring every 5 minutes, for 20 minutes or until sausage is cooked through. Remove and discard the bay leaf.

4. Remove the sausage and slice on the bias into 1-inch pieces. Stir sausage back into pan to reheat, then transfer everything to a large serving dish. Serve immediately with Italian bread as an option for making sandwiches or mopping up all the sauce.

SERVES 4 AS A SMALL PLATE
ACTIVE TIME = 45 MINUTES

———————★———————

3 tablespoons canola oil

1 pound spicy Italian sausage, in casing (best from an Italian specialty market)

½ cup thinly shaved Spanish yellow onion

1 cup thinly sliced red bell pepper

1 cup thinly sliced yellow bell pepper

1 teaspoon kosher salt

1 bay leaf

½ cup water

2 tablespoons ketchup

Loaf of Italian bread (optional)

———————★———————

USE A MANDOLINE TO THINLY SHAVE PEPPERS AND ONION.

Spareribs with Italian Plum Glaze

SERVES 4 AS A SMALL PLATE

ACTIVE TIME = 1 HOUR, 30 MINUTES

INACTIVE TIME = 2 HOURS

———— ★ ————

2 tablespoons canola oil

3 pounds spareribs, cut into 4 equal portions

1 teaspoon kosher salt

1 teaspoon freshly cracked black pepper

1 cup thinly sliced onion

¼ cup thinly sliced garlic

1 cup dry red wine

½ cup balsamic vinegar

½ cup plus ½ cup plum preserves

1 quart chicken broth

2 tablespoons Worcestershire sauce

6 sprigs thyme

2 cinnamon sticks (about 2 inches each)

2 bay leaves

2 tablespoons black peppercorns

Spareribs are a great cut, and not only because they're inexpensive. They're close to the pig's belly, which means there's a little more fat on them. That helps them stay tender when they're being cooked. The plum glaze here is sweet, to balance the salt.

1. Preheat the oven to 350°F.

2. Heat the canola oil in a large, heavy-bottomed pot (oven-safe) or Dutch oven over medium-high heat. Season the ribs with salt and pepper. Sear the meaty side of the ribs for 1½–2 minutes or until golden brown and set aside.

3. Lower the heat to medium and add onions and garlic. Sweat for 2 minutes and add the wine, balsamic vinegar, and ½ cup plum preserves. Simmer for 15–20 minutes, or until the liquid has reduced by half.

4. Add the chicken broth, Worcestershire sauce, thyme, cinnamon sticks, bay leaves, and peppercorns. Bring to a low boil and return the ribs to the pot. Cover with lid and braise in the oven for 2 hours or until the meat is tender and pulls away from the bone.

5. Remove from the oven and let the ribs cool slightly, keeping the oven on. Take out the ribs and set aside on a baking sheet at room temperature.

6. Strain the liquid through a fine-mesh strainer into a large, heatproof bowl or saucepan. Skim off and dis-

card the fat. Return the liquid to the heavy-bottomed pot and cook over medium-high heat. Simmer for 30 minutes to reduce the liquid by two-thirds and stir in the remaining ½ cup plum preserves. Simmer and reduce 5–10 minutes longer or until the liquid is syrupy.

7. Brush the reduced liquid onto the meat side of the ribs and bake for 10 minutes. Brush on more glaze, and bake 5 minutes longer. Transfer the ribs to a serving dish and serve with the remaining plum glaze on the side.

Spiced Pork Loin with Pumpkin Seed Sauce

SERVES 4 AS A SMALL PLATE

ACTIVE TIME = 80–90 MINUTES

INACTIVE TIME = 4 HOURS

———— ★ ————

BRINE AND PORK LOIN

2 cinnamon sticks

2 tablespoons black peppercorns

1 tablespoon whole allspice

1 teaspoon cumin seeds

½ teaspoon whole cloves

2 quarts water

1 cup kosher salt

½ cup garlic cloves, smashed

¼ cup light brown sugar

10 bay leaves

6 sprigs thyme

1 pound boneless pork loin

3 tablespoons canola oil

SPICE RUB

2 teaspoons slivered almonds

2 teaspoons sesame seeds

1 teaspoon cumin seeds

(INGREDIENTS CONTINUE NEXT PAGE)

The garlic, bay, cumin, and thyme in this brine infuse the pork with such big flavor. The pumpkin seed sauce adds a bit of heat and nice texture to the finished dish. This is one of those recipes where you just read down the list of ingredients and can practically smell the finished product.

1. To prepare the brine, toast the cinnamon sticks, peppercorns, allspice, cumin, and cloves in a dry sauté pan over medium heat for 5 minutes, shaking the pan often to prevent burning.

2. Transfer the spices to a large saucepan and add water, salt, garlic, brown sugar, bay leaves, and thyme. Bring to a boil, stirring to dissolve salt and sugar. Remove from heat and let cool completely. You can cool it more quickly by refrigerating it or by placing the saucepan of brine into a sink full of ice and stirring the brine to cool it.

3. Put the pork loin in a large, resealable freezer bag and place the bag in a deep dish to prevent leaking. Pour the chilled brine over the pork loin and seal the bag. Refrigerate for 4 hours; do not brine longer than that.

4. To prepare the spice rub, toast the almonds, sesame seeds, cumin seeds, peppercorns, and clove in a dry sauté pan over medium heat for 5 minutes, shaking

the pan often to prevent burning. Transfer to a spice grinder and add the pepitas and bread crumbs. Grind into a coarse powder and stir together with salt and brown sugar. Set aside.

5. To prepare the *Pumpkin Seed Sauce*, heat the canola oil in a large sauté pan over medium heat and sweat the shallots, garlic, and jalapeño for 4–5 minutes or until soft and translucent. Transfer to a food processor.

6. Add the pepitas, parsley, cilantro, and lemon juice to the food processor. Process while slowly adding the olive oil and water. Process for 30 seconds more. Transfer the mixture to a bowl, cover, and refrigerate. When the pork is finished brining, bring the sauce back up to room temperature.

7. Preheat the oven to 375°F. Remove the pork loin from the brine and rinse under cold running water. Pat dry with paper towels and fully coat it with the spice rub.

8. Heat the canola oil in a large oven-safe sauté pan over medium-high heat. Sear the pork loin on both sides for 4 minutes or until golden brown. Then, sear the rounded fat back.

9. Return the loin to a flat side, pour out any excess oil, and place the pan in the oven for 10–12 minutes or until the internal temperature of the meat reaches 140°F. Remove from the oven and let rest for 5–7 minutes.

10. Spoon the pumpkin seed sauce onto a large serving dish. Slice the pork into ¼-inch slices, layer them over one another atop the sauce, and serve.

½ teaspoon black peppercorns

1 clove

2 teaspoons roasted and salted pepitas

2 teaspoons panko bread crumbs

1½ teaspoons kosher salt

1½ teaspoons light brown sugar

PUMPKIN SEED SAUCE

1 tablespoon canola oil

½ cup small-diced shallots

1 tablespoon minced garlic

1 tablespoon small-diced jalapeño

1 cup roasted and salted pepitas

¼ cup flat-leaf Italian parsley, loosely packed

¼ cup cilantro, loosely packed

2 tablespoons lemon juice

1 tablespoon extra virgin olive oil

¼ cup water

———— ★ ————

PEPITAS ARE THE EDIBLE PART OF THE PUMPKIN SEED. THEY'RE FLAT, NARROW, AND GREEN IN COLOR.

11 lamb, lamb, goat

WE DEFINITELY HAD a wide variety of foods in our house growing up. My sister wasn't an adventurous eater at all, but I was always up for trying something new and different.

My mother's dietary choices meant we ate a lot of Mediterranean foods, because they were vegetarian-friendly cuisines. However, I also grew up eating lamb because it was typically the only red meat my mom brought into the house. Whenever we'd say to her, "Ma, you're a vegetarian—how can you eat red meat?" she'd say, "It's not red meat, it's lamb." I also remember eating curried goat as a kid.

They may not qualify as vegetarian, exactly, but preparing lamb and goat at home is really easy, and these meats are so full of flavor. As with many ingredients, getting to know the meat purveyors at your local farmers' market is a great way to find really fresh lamb and goat.

Braised Leg of Lamb with Fermented Greek-Style Couscous and Tomato

SERVES 6 AS A SMALL PLATE

ACTIVE TIME = 35–40 MINUTES

INACTIVE TIME = 4 HOURS

———— ★ ————

3-pound leg of lamb

1 tablespoon kosher salt

2 teaspoons freshly cracked black pepper

3 tablespoons canola oil

2 cups thinly sliced onions

1 cup thinly sliced garlic

2 tablespoons tomato paste

2 cups canned crushed tomatoes

1 quart chicken broth

10 sprigs thyme

1 bay leaf

3½ cups *Fermented Greek-Style Couscous* (recipe follows)

1 tablespoon lemon juice

In Greece, you can buy this fermented couscous—trahana—in specialty stores, but I learned how to make my own, and I've been doing it ever since. It's a little sweet, a little sour, but hearty all the way around. Serving it with braised leg of lamb is a holiday tradition. If you don't have time to make your own, you can make this dish with regular couscous. I hope you'll try making the fermented couscous at least once, though. It's really easy to do and tastes so much better.

1. Preheat the oven to 325°F.

2. Using a meat cleaver, cut the leg of lamb at the joint into two pieces and season with salt and pepper. Heat the canola oil in a large, heavy-bottomed pot (oven safe) over medium-high heat. Sear the lamb for 2 minutes on every side until golden brown. Remove the lamb from the pot and let it rest on a cutting board.

3. Lower the heat to medium and sauté onions and garlic for 3–4 minutes, until the garlic is golden.

4. Stir in the tomato paste and sauté for 1 minute. Add the crushed tomatoes and sauté for 5 minutes, stirring often. Add the chicken broth, thyme, and bay leaf. Bring the mixture to a low boil and add the lamb. Cover with a

MAKES 3½ CUPS

ACTIVE TIME = 40–45 MINUTES

INACTIVE TIME = 8 DAYS

———— ★ ————

FERMENTED GREEK-STYLE COUSCOUS

1 quart whole milk (divided)

2 teaspoons plain Greek yogurt

1 tablespoon lemon juice

1 tablespoon kosher salt

2 cups cracked bulgur wheat

lid and braise in the oven for 4 hours, turning the meat every hour. When done, the meat should be falling off the bone.

5. Remove from oven and let the lamb rest in the liquid for 15 minutes.

6. Take the lamb out of the liquid and let it rest on a cutting board. Skim and discard the fat from the liquid's surface. Stir the fermented couscous and lemon juice into the braising liquid, and cook on the stovetop over medium heat for 5 minutes. The couscous will absorb some of the liquid, but not all of it. That's okay—a thick, soupy consistency is what you want.

7. Break the lamb into big pieces, discarding the fatty parts. Transfer the couscous to a large serving dish, top with lamb, and serve.

Fermented Greek-Style Couscous

1. Stir together 1 cup milk and yogurt in large mixing bowl (at least 2-quart in size). Cover it with cheesecloth and wrap it tightly with kitchen twine. Keep the bowl on the countertop at room temperature for 1 day, stirring twice during that 24-hour period. When you're not stirring, the bowl should remain covered with cheesecloth and tied shut.

2. After 1 day, stir in another 1 cup milk. Keep the bowl on the countertop at room temperature for another day, stirring twice during that 24-hour period. Again, when not stirring, the bowl should remain covered with cheesecloth and tied shut.

3. Repeat with the remaining 2 cups milk, adding 1 cup per day and keeping the bowl covered and at room temperature.

4. After the fourth day, add the now-soured milk mixture, lemon juice, and salt to a large saucepan and bring to a low boil. Whisk in the bulgur wheat a quarter-cup at a time. The mixture will become thick. Lower the heat to low and simmer for 20–25 minutes, stirring often to prevent scorching.

5. Line a large colander with dampened cheesecloth and place it in a baking dish or pan to catch any liquid that seeps through. Transfer the mixture to the colander. Cover with dampened cheesecloth and keep the bowl on the countertop at room temperature for 4 more days. The cheesecloth will dry out; that's okay.

6. Using your hands, break apart the fermented couscous and crumble into very small pieces. Store it in a sealed container in the refrigerator for up to 1 week.

Crispy Baby Goat with Goat Cheese Polenta

Baby goat is readily available in the early summertime. If you get to know your farmers and butchers, they'll hold the best cuts for you.

1. Preheat the oven to 325°F.

2. Place the goat in a large, oven-safe, heavy-bottomed pot and pour in canola oil. Cover with lid and oil-poach for 2 hours.

3. To prepare the polenta, bring the water, milk, and salt to a slight boil over medium-high heat. Whisk in the polenta, lower the heat to low, and cook on a low simmer for 45–50 minutes, stirring often with a wooden spoon. The polenta will become very thick and creamy. Stir in the butter and goat cheese until fully melted into the polenta. Add a little water if it seems too thick. Polenta can be kept on low heat until ready to serve.

4. Remove the goat from the oven and let cool at room temperature for 15 minutes. Take it out of the oil and break it into large pieces.

5. Spoon 2 tablespoons canola oil from the pot into a large sauté pan and cook over medium-high heat. Sear each piece of goat on both sides for 2–3 minutes or until crispy.

6. Whisk the polenta before transferring it to a large serving dish. Top with goat, drizzle it with saba, and finish with mint and sea salt.

SERVES 4 AS A SMALL PLATE
ACTIVE TIME = 1 HOUR
INACTIVE TIME = 1 HOUR

———— ★ ————

1 pound baby goat shoulder (boneless)

1 quart canola oil

3 cups water

2 cups whole milk

1 teaspoon kosher salt

1 cup dry polenta

2 tablespoons unsalted butter

4 ounces goat cheese, crumbled

1 tablespoon saba

12 mint leaves, torn

¼ teaspoon sea salt (Maldon recommended)

———— ★ ————

SABA IS A CONCENTRATED SYRUP MADE FROM FRESHLY SQUEEZED GRAPE JUICE. ALSO KNOWN AS "GRAPE MUST," IT IS SWEETER AND LESS ACIDIC THAN BALSAMIC VINEGAR. FIND SABA ONLINE OR IN A SPECIALTY ITALIAN MARKET.

Goat Shoulder Braised in Goat's Milk

SERVES 4 AS A SMALL PLATE

ACTIVE TIME = 40–45 MINUTES

INACTIVE TIME = 2 HOURS

———————★———————

1½ pounds goat shoulder (boneless), cut into 2-inch cubes

1 tablespoon kosher salt

1½ teaspoons freshly cracked black pepper

2 tablespoons canola oil

½ cup small-diced onions

1 tablespoon minced garlic

5 cardamom pods

1 tablespoon unsalted butter

2 tablespoons all-purpose flour

3 cups chicken broth

1 cup goat milk

3 sprigs thyme

1 bay leaf

Braising meat in milk has been done for generations, and because goat milk has light, salty undertones, it helps flavor the goat shoulder naturally. The goat will break apart nicely at the end, and I suggest serving it (along with the hot braising milk) over pasta or gnocchi, or even polenta.

1. Preheat the oven to 325°F.

2. Season the goat with salt and pepper. Heat the canola oil in a large, oven-safe, heavy-bottomed pot over medium-high heat and sear the goat for 2 minutes on all sides until golden brown. Remove the goat from the pot and let rest on a cutting board at room temperature.

3. Lower the heat to medium and add onions and garlic to the pot. Sauté for 3–5 minutes, until the garlic is golden.

4. In a small, dry sauté pan, toast the cardamom pods over medium heat for 3 minutes, shaking the pan often to prevent burning. Set aside.

5. Add the butter to the onions. When melted, whisk in the flour for 3–4 minutes to create a roux. Add the chicken broth, goat milk, thyme, bay leaf, toasted cardamom, and seared goat shoulder. Increase the heat to bring mixture to a low boil, cover with lid and braise in the oven for 2 hours or until goat is tender.

6. Remove from oven and let the goat rest in the liquid for 15 minutes. Take out the goat and let it rest on a cutting board at room temperature.

7. Pour the braising liquid through a fine-mesh strainer into a blender and blend for 2 minutes or until emulsified. Return the liquid and goat to the pot over medium-high heat. Bring to a simmer, stirring to break up the goat a little bit.

8. Transfer to a large serving bowl and serve.

Goat Cheese Gnudi with Basil, Prosciutto, and Tomato

SERVES 4 AS A SMALL PLATE

ACTIVE TIME = 90 MINUTES

--------------- ★ ---------------

¾ cup ricotta cheese

¾ cup goat cheese, room temperature

1 large egg

1 egg yolk

¼ teaspoon plus 1 teaspoon kosher salt

½ cup all-purpose flour, plus more for dusting

8 plum tomatoes

¼ cup extra virgin olive oil

½ cup small-diced shallot

3 sprigs thyme

6 medium basil leaves, torn

2 ounces prosciutto, torn

Gnudi literally means "naked," and in Italian cooking, it means the filling for pasta like ravioli, but without the pasta. Gnudi are little dumplings that look like gnocchi, but instead are very light on flour and heavier on everything else.

1. In the bowl of a stand mixer fitted with the paddle, combine the cheeses, egg, egg yolk, and ¼ teaspoon salt. Mix on the lowest speed until just combined. With mixer still on low speed, slowly add ½ cup flour. Mix for 30 seconds, or until just combined.

2. Dust your hands with flour and form the mixture into 1-inch balls, flatten slightly, and dust with flour. Arrange the gnudi on a flour-dusted baking sheet, making sure they don't touch each other. Refrigerate for 1 hour.

3. To prepare the tomato sauce, bring a large pot of water to a boil. Set a bowl of ice water to the side. Using a paring knife, score the tomatoes on stem and bottom ends, making a shallow "X." Blanch the tomatoes for 2 minutes and shock in ice water until chilled. Remove and discard the skins.

4. Cut the tomatoes into quarters. Remove and discard the pulp and seeds. Purée tomato flesh in a food processor for 1 minute.

5. Bring a separate large pot of salted water to a boil for the gnudi.

6. Meanwhile, heat the olive oil in a large saucepan over medium-low heat and sweat the shallot and thyme for 20–25 minutes, stirring occasionally or until shallots are very soft. Remove and discard the thyme. Increase heat to medium-high and stir in tomato purée and remaining teaspoon of salt. Bring to a low boil, then lower heat to medium-low and simmer for 12 minutes. The sauce can be kept at room temperature until ready to serve.

7. Once the pot of salted water is boiling, gently add the gnudi in batches, being careful not to overcrowd the pot. Cook for 2–3 minutes, or until they float. Remove with a slotted spoon or wok skimmer and set aside in a single layer.

8. Reheat the tomato sauce and spoon it into a large serving dish, top with gnudi, and garnish with basil and prosciutto.

Three-Day Marinated Rack of Lamb

Lamb tastes best when served medium-rare, and this marinade brings out incredible flavor. Ask your butcher or person working the meat counter to french the rack of lamb for you.

1. Blend lemon juice, rosemary, thyme, and oregano in a blender on medium speed. With blender running, slowly stream in both oils.

2. Cut racks of lamb into 1-bone chops and arrange in a glass baking dish in a single layer. Pour the marinade over the meat and cover with plastic wrap. Refrigerate for 3 days.

3. Remove lamb from refrigerator and season with salt.

4. Heat an outdoor grill or indoor grill pan to medium-high. Grill the chops for 2 minutes on each side to medium rare. Serve immediately.

SERVES 4 AS A SMALL PLATE
ACTIVE TIME = 30–35 MINUTES
INACTIVE TIME = 3 DAYS

———————★———————

½ cup lemon juice

1 tablespoon rosemary

1 tablespoon thyme

1 tablespoon dried oregano

1½ cups canola oil

½ cup extra virgin olive oil

2 racks of lamb, cleaned and frenched (New Zealand lamb recommended)

2 teaspoons kosher salt

Lamb Meatballs with Spicy Tomato Sauce

SERVES 4 AS A SMALL PLATE;
MAKES APPROXIMATELY
16 MEATBALLS
ACTIVE TIME = 45–50 MINUTES

———— ★ ————

1 tablespoon cumin seeds

3 tablespoons plus 1 cup extra virgin olive oil

½ cup minced yellow onion

2 tablespoons minced garlic

⅛ teaspoon red chili flakes

2 slices white bread, crust removed

½ cup whole milk

1 large egg

½ pound ground lamb

½ pound ground beef (80/20 preferred)

¼ cup small-diced green, pitted olives

1½ teaspoons kosher salt

1 teaspoon ground black pepper

(INGREDIENTS CONTINUE NEXT PAGE)

When rolling the meatballs by hand, be careful not to overwork the meat. You don't want the meatballs to be too dense. Have a candy thermometer ready to check the oil's temperature just before pan-frying these meatballs.

1. Toast the cumin seeds in a small, dry sauté pan over medium heat for 5 minutes, shaking the pan often to prevent burning. Transfer the seeds to a spice grinder and grind into a powder. Set aside.

2. Heat 3 tablespoons olive oil in a large sauté pan over medium heat. Sweat the onions for 4–5 minutes, or until soft and translucent. Add the garlic and sauté for 2 minutes. Add the ground cumin and chili flakes and cook for 1 minute longer. Transfer to a large mixing bowl to cool to room temperature.

3. Soak the bread in the milk, then squeeze excess milk out of the bread. Mince the bread.

4. Add the minced bread, egg, ground meats, olives, salt, and pepper to the onion and garlic mixture. Mix with your hands until all ingredients are incorporated.

5. Roll the meat mixture into 1-ounce balls, or slightly smaller than golf balls.

6. In a large saucepan over medium heat, stir hot cherry peppers into the tomato sauce and heat through. In a

separate large sauté pan, bring the canola oil and remaining 1 cup olive oil to 300°F over medium-high heat.

7. Pan-fry meatballs for 3 minutes, then turn over and cook for 3 minutes longer. Remove meatballs from oil and drain on paper towels.

8. Transfer the spicy tomato sauce to a large serving bowl and top with lamb meatballs. Garnish with feta cheese and dill. Serve immediately.

2 cups *The "Grand Mother" Tomato Sauce* **(page 134)**

2 tablespoons minced tangy, hot cherry peppers (found in the pickle and olive aisle of your grocery store)

1 cup canola oil

¼ cup crumbled feta cheese

1 tablespoon chopped dill

Marinated Lamb Kabob with Yogurt and Dill Pesto

I use top round lamb in this recipe because it's the best piece of the lamb leg for making kabobs. It's a small cut—usually 1 or 2 pounds—and it's incredibly tender with great flavor.

1. Toast the cumin seeds in a dry sauté pan over medium heat for 5 minutes, shaking the pan often to prevent burning. Transfer to a spice grinder and grind into a powder.

2. In a mixing bowl, combine the ground cumin, yogurt, olive oil, lemon juice, and ¼ teaspoon salt.

3. Put the lamb in a glass baking dish, pour the yogurt marinade over the meat, and toss to coat. Cover and refrigerate for at least 4 hours or overnight.

4. Remove the lamb from the refrigerator 15 minutes before you're ready to cook. Spear the lamb onto skewers, blotting any excess yogurt with a paper towel.

5. Heat an outdoor grill (or indoor grill pan) to medium-high. Season lamb with the remaining salt. Grill the lamb for 2 minutes, turn over, and grill for 1 minute longer. Serve with *Dill Pesto* on the side.

SERVES 4 AS A SMALL PLATE
ACTIVE TIME = 35–40 MINUTES
INACTIVE TIME = 4 HOURS

————★————

2 teaspoons cumin seeds

½ cup plain Greek yogurt

1 tablespoon extra virgin olive oil

2 teaspoons lemon juice

¼ teaspoon plus 1¾ teaspoons kosher salt

1 pound top round lamb; cut into 1 x ½-inch pieces

4 bamboo skewers, soaked in water

½ cup *Dill Pesto* (recipe follows)

Dill Pesto

MAKES APPROXIMATELY ½ CUP
ACTIVE TIME = 15–20 MINUTES

———————★———————

2 tablespoons walnuts

2 cups dill, tightly packed

¼ cup grated kefalograviera
cheese (Greek cheese similar to
Parmigiano-Reggiano)

1 teaspoon minced garlic

½ teaspoon kosher salt

⅓ cup extra virgin olive oil

———————★———————

PESTO CAN BE REFRIGERATED
FOR UP TO 3 DAYS. THIS PESTO IS
MEANT TO BE A LITTLE "BROKEN"
IN THAT IT WILL SEPARATE
SLIGHTLY. JUST WHISK IT FOR A
FEW SECONDS TO BRING IT BACK
TOGETHER BEFORE SERVING.

1. Toast the walnuts in a dry sauté pan for 5 minutes over medium heat, shaking the pan often to prevent burning.

2. In a food processor, combine the toasted walnuts, dill, kefalograviera cheese, garlic, and salt. Process while slowly adding the olive oil until a paste forms, approximately 30–45 seconds. You may need to stop and scrape down the sides of your food processor to incorporate all the ingredients.

Slow-Roasted Goat with Greek Salad

So simple, so flavorful.

1. Preheat the oven to 300°F. Season the goat with salt.

2. Place a baking rack on a baking sheet and arrange the thyme, rosemary, and bay leaves on the rack. Place the goat on the herbs and roast in the oven for 30 minutes or until the meat reaches an internal temperature of 125°F.

3. Toss all the salad ingredients in a large mixing bowl. Transfer the salad to a large serving dish.

4. Remove the goat from the oven and let it rest at room temperature for 4 minutes. Slice into ½-inch pieces and lay them on the salad. Garnish with feta and serve.

SERVES 4 AS A SMALL PLATE

ACTIVE TIME = 35–40 MINUTES

———— ★ ————

GOAT

1 pound goat tenderloin (3–4 loins) or lamb tenderloin

2 teaspoons kosher salt

8 sprigs thyme

3 sprigs rosemary

4 bay leaves

¼ cup crumbled feta cheese

SALAD

1 cup chopped plum tomatoes

1 cup chopped English cucumber

½ cup medium-diced green bell pepper

½ cup medium-diced red onion

1 tablespoon dried oregano

¼ cup extra virgin olive oil

3 tablespoons red wine vinegar

1 teaspoon kosher salt

Slow-Roasted Lamb Shank with Olive Pesto

SERVES 4 AS A SMALL PLATE

ACTIVE TIME = 15 MINUTES

INACTIVE TIME = 2 HOURS

———— ★ ————

1 cup rough-chopped onion

½ cup chopped carrot

½ cup chopped celery

10 sprigs thyme

3½ pounds lamb shanks, bone-in (approximately 4–5 shanks)

2 tablespoons kosher salt

½ cup *Olive Pesto* (recipe follows)

¼ teaspoon sea salt (Maldon recommended)

Slow roasting meat means less moisture is lost, resulting in a more tender dish. Here, the meat will not be falling off the bone, and it will be similar in feel to sliced roast beef. Make sure you have a working meat thermometer to check the internal temperature of the lamb as it cooks.

1. Preheat oven to 300°F.

2. Put onions, carrots, celery, and thyme in a roasting pan. Season the lamb with salt and place on top of the vegetables.

3. Roast for 1 hour. Flip the shanks and roast for 1 hour longer or until meat reaches an internal temperature of 130°F.

4. Remove the lamb from oven and let it rest at room temperature for 7 minutes. Thinly slice the meat off the bone and arrange it on a serving dish. Top with *Olive Pesto* and finish with sea salt.

Olive Pesto

1. In a food processor, combine the roasted garlic, olives, pistachios, tarragon, orange zest, orange juice, and capers. Process while slowly adding the olive oil until a paste forms, approximately 30–45 seconds. You may need to stop and scrape down the sides of the food processor bowl to incorporate all the ingredients.

MAKES APPROXIMATELY ¾ CUP
ACTIVE TIME = 2 MINUTES

———————★———————

2 cloves *Roasted Garlic* (page 62)

1 cup pitted Kalamata olives

3 tablespoons roasted, shelled pistachios

2 tablespoons tarragon leaves, lightly packed

Zest of ½ orange

1 teaspoon orange juice

1 teaspoon capers

¼ cup extra virgin olive oil

———————★———————

PESTO CAN BE REFRIGERATED FOR UP TO 1 WEEK.

12 sweet memories

ECAUSE WE DIDN'T have a lot of money growing up, my mom, sister, and I would make cookies for family members for the holidays. Although my sister didn't like to cook, she loved to bake, so it was an activity we could all do together. We made a lot of different kinds of cookies and cakes, but the one I remember most was Rainbow Cookies—you know, the ones that look like the Italian flag: red, white, and green. We made them every Christmas Eve day. They were easy to make with almond paste, flour, butter, and food coloring, layered with jam, and topped with chocolate.

One Christmas Day when we were driving to my aunt's house, my mom kept hearing the crinkle of plastic wrap in the backseat of the car and asked, "What's going on back there?"

"Nothin'," I'd reply, my mouth full of cookies. When we got to my aunt's house and mom presented her with this beautiful tray of cookies as a gift, I'm sure she noticed the big spaces where all the rainbow cookies once were and the chocolate icing in the corners of my mouth. But no one said a word.

These days, I like desserts that play salt off sweet. I also like desserts with aromatics, like rosemary and juniper. In my kitchens, I encourage my chefs and cooks to come up with desserts that are inventive and creative, but that mean something. I want the last thing you eat before leaving my restaurant to be just as good and exciting as the first bite you took.

Aunt Norma's Christmas Peanut Brittle

MAKES JUST OVER 2.5 POUNDS OF
BRITTLE, OR 8 CUPS.
ACTIVE TIME = 30 MINUTES
INACTIVE TIME = 30 MINUTES

——————★——————

2 cups sugar

1 cup light corn syrup

1 cup water

1 stick (8 tablespoons) unsalted butter

1 pound raw peanuts

2 teaspoons baking soda

1 teaspoon vanilla extract

My Aunt Norma made peanut brittle for the holidays, and I still love it. I've included her recipe here, as well as a revised version for how I like to make it now. One note about peanut brittle: don't try to make it on rainy, warm, humid days. It won't harden or set. The same goes for hot summer days.

1. Grease a shallow jellyroll pan or 13 x 18-inch sheet pan with butter or nonstick spray, or line it with a Silpat.

2. In a large, heavy-bottomed pot fitted with a candy thermometer, heat the sugar, corn syrup, and water to 220°F over medium-high heat. Stir to dissolve the sugar and keep stirring occasionally as the mixture heats to 220°F.

3. Add the butter and peanuts and stir continuously until mixture reaches 300°F.

4. Remove from heat, take out the thermometer, and quickly and vigorously stir in the baking soda and vanilla extract.

5. Pour the mixture evenly onto the baking sheet and let cool at room temperature for at least 30 minutes. Once cooled, break the brittle into pieces.

Mike's Brittle

I love Aunt Norma's brittle, and over the years, I've come up with another version I think you might like.

→ Before you start, cut 6 slices of thick-cut bacon into ¼-inch pieces. Sauté over medium-high heat until nice and crispy. Drain on paper towels.

→ Swap in ½ pound pine nuts for half the peanuts.

→ Add the cooked bacon along with zest of 1 orange in Step 4. Finish as usual.

Fresh Waffle Cone with Pistachio Gelato, Like I Had When I Was a Kid

MAKES 4–6 CONES

ACTIVE TIME = 10–15 MINUTES

——————— ★ ———————

CONES

⅓ cup sugar

2 tablespoons butter, melted

2 large egg whites

⅔ cup all-purpose flour

Pinch of salt

½ teaspoon vanilla extract

Pistachio Gelato (recipe follows)

——————— ★ ———————

THIS RECIPE REQUIRES TWO PIECES OF SPECIAL EQUIPMENT—A PIZZELLE IRON AND AN ICE CREAM MAKER. YOU SHOULD BE ABLE TO FIND BOTH THESE THINGS IN A MAJOR DEPARTMENT STORE OR KITCHEN GOODS STORE, AND YOU CAN DEFINITELY FIND THEM ONLINE.

My parents got divorced when I was three years old. When I was six or seven, I sometimes got to go into Manhattan with my dad. So, I'd get dressed up in my little dress pants and a tie and go into the city with him. We'd walk down the halls of his office together, and I felt like such a cool tough guy. He'd take me out to lunch, and afterward we'd go to this street cart where they made these little skinny waffle cones called pizzelles. The guy would press the batter on the thin waffle iron, then bend it around to make a fresh cone. You'd smell it a block away.

While the cone was still warm, he put in this big scoop of pistachio gelato . . . and so the gelato started to melt, and it dripped all over my dress shirt and good pants, but it didn't matter because it tasted so good and I was there with my dad. That memory has stuck with me for thirty years.

When I think back on it, there were probably other gelato flavors I could've had—chocolate, vanilla, strawberry—but I chose pistachio because it was green and I thought that was cool. Eating that des-

sert—sticky, sweet, and so fragrant—is just some-thing I'll never forget.

1. In a mixing bowl, whisk together the sugar and but-ter. One at a time, whisk in the egg whites, flour, salt, and vanilla, until all are just combined. Don't overmix.

2. Preheat a pizzelle iron according to the manufac-turer's instructions. Drop rounded spoonfuls of bat-ter onto the iron. Close and cook for about 90 seconds, or until steam stops coming out of the iron. Carefully remove the thin waffle and form it around the cone shaper that comes with the iron. Cones can be stored in an airtight container at room temperature.

Pistachio Gelato

1. In a large saucepan, bring the milk, cream, ¼ cup sugar, cardamom, and orange zest to a low boil over medium heat. Lower the heat to a simmer.

2. In a separate bowl, whisk together the remaining ¼ cup sugar with the egg yolks and pistachio paste.

3. Temper the yolk mixture by whisking in a half-cup of the hot milk mixture, then add the tempered yolk mix-ture to the hot milk. Return to a simmer over medium heat, stirring with a wooden spoon until it thickens and coats the back of the spoon.

4. Pour the mixture through a fine-mesh strainer into a heatproof bowl and refrigerate for 4 hours.

5. Freeze the mixture in an ice cream maker according to the manufacturer's instructions.

MAKES APPROXIMATELY 4 CUPS

ACTIVE TIME = 20 MINUTES

INACTIVE TIME = 4 HOURS

———————★———————

PISTACHIO GELATO

2½ cups whole milk

1 cup heavy cream

¼ cup plus ¼ cup sugar

2 cardamom pods

Zest of ½ orange

4 large egg yolks

2 tablespoons pistachio paste

Nutella Cookie Sandwiches

MAKES 45–50 COOKIE SANDWICHES
ACTIVE TIME = 1 HOUR

———————★———————

½ cup light brown sugar, packed

½ cup sugar

1 cup Nutella, plus more for filling

2 sticks unsalted butter, room temperature

2½ cups all-purpose flour, plus more for dusting

2 teaspoons kosher salt

2 teaspoons baking soda

¼ cup raw sugar

———————★———————

FOR PERFECT ROOM-TEMPERATURE BUTTER, LEAVE THE BUTTER ON YOUR COUNTERTOP FOR 2–6 HOURS TO COMPLETELY SOFTEN.

I don't know anyone who doesn't like Nutella, that perfect chocolate-hazelnut spread. These cookie sandwiches are great little bites at the end of a meal, and they also make great birthday party treats or holiday gifts.

1. Preheat oven to 325°F. Have two nonstick baking sheets ready or line baking sheets with parchment paper.

2. In the bowl of a stand mixer fitted with the paddle attachment, mix the brown sugar, sugar, and Nutella on the second-lowest speed for 1 minute or until the ingredients are fully incorporated. Add the butter and mix on the third-lowest speed for 2 minutes, or until whipped and light in color.

3. In a separate bowl, whisk together the flour, salt, and baking soda. Slowly add the flour mixture to the mixer on the lowest speed setting. Mix all ingredients for 2 minutes, stopping halfway through to scrape down the inside of the mixing bowl to incorporate all the ingredients. The dough will come together and pull away from the sides of the mixing bowl. It will look a little crumbly—that's okay.

4. Dust a work surface and rolling pin with flour to prevent sticking. With your hands, scoop out one-third of the dough and mold it into a small brick on your work surface. Rolling from the center out—"north, south, east, and west"—gently roll the dough into a ¹⁄₁₆-inch-

thick sheet. Dust the surface of the dough with a little flour before rolling. If the dough starts to tear or stick to the rolling pin, dust with a little more flour.

COOKIES CAN BE REFRIGERATED FOR UP TO 5 DAYS.

5. Using a 2-inch ring mold or 2-inch circular cookie cutter, punch out cookies and place them on nonstick or parchment-lined baking sheets.

6. Add some dough from the mixing bowl to what's left over on your work surface and pull it together and roll like you did in Step 4. Punch out more cookies and repeat until all the dough has been used.

7. Placing the cookie sheets on the middle and lower oven racks, bake the cookies for 5 minutes, remove them from the oven, and sprinkle evenly with raw sugar. Put the cookies back in the oven, rotating the baking sheets 180 degrees, and switching the upper and lower cookie sheet positions so they bake evenly for 5 more minutes.

8. Remove the cookies from the oven, let rest on the baking sheet for 1 minute, and use a clean offset spatula to transfer them to a cooling rack.

9. When cooled, fill a piping bag (or Ziploc bag with the corner snipped off) with Nutella. Pipe 1½ teaspoons on the flat surface of half the cookies, and top with the remaining cookies. Refrigerate in a sealed container for 1 hour before serving.

Honey-Soaked Cookies

I used to make these cookies when I was executive chef at Zaytinya in Washington, D.C. They're based on a traditional Greek pastry called finikia, where the orange and cinnamon are prominent.

1. Preheat oven to 350°F.

2. In the bowl of a stand mixer fitted with the paddle attachment, mix the olive oil, orange zest, orange juice, cognac, and 3 tablespoons sugar on medium speed for 3 minutes.

3. In a separate bowl, whisk together the flour, cinnamon, clove, and baking soda.

4. Turn the mixer speed to low and slowly add the flour mixture. Mix on low for 2 minutes, or until a soft dough forms.

5. Scoop 2-teaspoon portions of dough and roll into balls. Place them 1 inch apart on nonstick or parchment-lined baking sheets.

6. Bake for 10 minutes, rotate the baking sheets 180 degrees, and bake 10 minutes longer. If baking two sheets at a time, switch their position on the racks as well when rotating them.

7. Bring the remaining sugar, water, and honey to a boil in a large saucepan over high heat. Lower the heat to medium and simmer for 5 minutes. Keep the mixture warm on low heat until the cookies finish baking.

MAKES APPROXIMATELY
36 COOKIES
ACTIVE TIME = 40–45 MINUTES

———————★———————

½ cup olive oil

Zest of ½ orange

3 tablespoons orange juice

1 tablespoon cognac

3 tablespoons plus ½ cup sugar

2½ cups cake flour

1½ teaspoons ground cinnamon

½ teaspoon ground clove

½ teaspoon baking soda

½ cup water

½ cup honey

½ cup finely chopped walnuts

8. In a dry sauté pan, toast the walnuts over medium heat for 5 minutes, shaking the pan often to prevent burning.

9. When the cookies are done baking, place them into the honey mixture and let them soak for 10 minutes. If they do not all fit, soak in batches. Remove and let rest on a baking rack.

10. Top with toasted walnuts. Cookies can be kept in a sealed container at room temperature for 3 days.

Fried Apple Pie Calzone

SERVES 4

ACTIVE TIME = 1 HOUR, 30 MINUTES

──────── ★ ────────

3 cups peeled, sliced Granny Smith apples

2 tablespoons all-purpose flour

½ teaspoon ground cinnamon

½ cup sugar

1 tablespoon unsalted butter

2 tablespoons bourbon

¼ cup water

4 *Pizza Dough* balls (page 106)

6 cups canola oil (quantity may vary depending on your deep fryer)

Use good-quality bourbon for this dessert—I like Knob Creek. You could serve this with vanilla ice cream, but it's great on its own.

1. Preheat the oven to 300°F.

2. Toss the apples with flour and cinnamon in a mixing bowl until evenly coated.

3. Add sugar to a heavy-bottomed pot over high heat. Do not stir. When it begins to brown around the edges, stir with a wooden spoon. When sugar has fully dissolved and is medium caramel in color, stir in the butter. When the butter is melted, carefully stir in the bourbon.

4. Add the apples and lower the heat to medium-low. Stir to evenly coat apples in caramel. If the caramel tightens, add a little water and continue to stir. Simmer on low heat for 5–7 minutes or until smooth in texture. Remove from heat and set aside to cool.

5. Onto a lightly flour-dusted surface, roll out each dough ball into an 8-inch circle. Dust with flour as needed to prevent sticking. On one half of each circle, spoon a quarter of the apple mixture. Leave ½ inch around the edge for sealing.

6. Fold over each calzone, creating a half-moon shape, and press out any air bubbles. Starting at one end, crimp the edges to seal each calzone so that no filling will leak out. Refrigerate for 15–30 minutes.

7. While the calzones are chilling, heat the canola oil in an electric deep fryer to 350°F. If you do not have an electric fryer, use a heavy-bottomed pot and a candy thermometer.

8. Deep-fry the calzones, one at a time, for 6–8 minutes each, or until golden brown. Place them on a baking rack over a baking sheet and keep them warm in the oven. Repeat with remaining calzones. Serve warm.

Rosemary Panna Cotta with Spiced Orange Compote and Pine Nuts

SERVES 4

ACTIVE TIME = 25–30 MINUTES

INACTIVE TIME = 4 HOURS

———————— ★ ————————

1 envelope unflavored gelatin
(¼ ounce)

3 tablespoons sugar

Pinch kosher salt

½ cup whole milk

Seeds of ¼ vanilla bean

1 sprig rosemary

1¾ cups plain Greek yogurt

1 teaspoon lemon juice

¾ cup *Spiced Orange Compote*
(recipe follows)

In culinary school, I learned how to make crème caramel, crème brûlée, and panna cotta because I'm a big fan of custard-based desserts. Before I went on Top Chef All-Stars, I practiced a lot of sweets, because that's the running joke on the show: that none of us ever seem ready or happy to make a dessert as part of a challenge. I worked on this rosemary panna cotta recipe for about a month before I went to tape the finale. Because I didn't have a restaurant of my own at the time, I worked in friends' restaurant kitchens to learn more about the pastry side of things.

I knew when I went to the All-Stars finale I wanted to use Italian flavors, but not necessarily sweets from my childhood. I memorized this recipe and went into the finale knowing I was going to do this dessert. Though it didn't earn me the big prize, renowned chef and finale judge Hubert Keller called it a "perfect dessert." That was enough for me.

1. In a small saucepan, combine the gelatin, sugar, salt, milk, vanilla bean seeds, and rosemary. Stir and let steep at room temperature for 3 minutes.

2. Bring the milk mixture to a simmer over medium heat. When small bubbles appear around the edge of the pan, whisk until the sugar, salt, and gelatin are dissolved.

3. Remove from heat and let cool for 5 minutes. Remove and discard the rosemary.

4. Pour the mixture into a blender. Add yogurt and lemon juice and blend for 20 seconds.

5. Divide the mixture evenly between four small custard or other dessert dishes. Cover with plastic wrap and chill for 4 hours or overnight.

6. Right before serving, remove the panna cotta from the refrigerator, invert it onto a plate to release it from its mold, and top with *Spiced Orange Compote*.

———★———

TO REMOVE SEEDS FROM THE VANILLA BEAN, USE A PARING KNIFE TO SLICE DOWN THE LENGTH OF THE BEAN TO OPEN IT UP. WITH THE OPEN BEAN STILL ON THE CUTTING BOARD, USE THE DULL EDGE OF YOUR PARING KNIFE TO SCRAPE OUT THE SEEDS, WHICH WILL LOOK LIKE A DARK BROWN CLUMP OF PASTE.

———★———

Spiced Orange Compote

1. Toast the pine nuts in a dry sauté pan over medium heat for 5 minutes, shaking the pan often to prevent burning. Set aside.

2. In a small saucepan, bring the sugar, honey, water, allspice, cloves, and cinnamon stick to a simmer over medium heat for 10 minutes, stirring occasionally, until it becomes syrup-like.

3. Strain and discard the spices. Return the liquid to the saucepan and add the orange segments and toasted pine nuts. Reduce the heat to low and simmer for 6–7 minutes longer, until the oranges are soft. Remove the compote from the heat and let it cool before spooning it onto the panna cotta.

MAKES APPROXIMATELY ¾ CUP
ACTIVE TIME = 20–25 MINUTES

———— ★ ————

2 tablespoons pine nuts

2 tablespoons sugar

2 tablespoons honey

2 tablespoons water

3 whole dried allspice berries

2 whole cloves

½ cinnamon stick

3 oranges, supremed segments only (page 39)

Nutella Pudding with Hazelnut Crumble and Grappa Cream

SERVES 4

ACTIVE TIME = 1 HOUR, 15 MINUTES

---- ★ ----

PUDDING

⅔ cup plus 2 cups whole milk

2 large egg yolks

¼ cup cornstarch

¾ cup sugar

½ pound bittersweet chocolate chips

½ cup Nutella

2 tablespoons unsalted butter

(INGREDIENTS CONTINUE NEXT PAGE)

Grappa is an Italian alcohol made by distilling pomace, the organic material left over from winemaking. Grappa is smooth, but strong, and brings a distinct flavor to the cream in this dessert.

1. In a large mixing bowl, whisk together ⅔ cup milk and egg yolks. Add the cornstarch sparingly while whisking to prevent clumping. Set aside.

2. Heat the remaining 2 cups milk and sugar in a medium saucepan over medium heat until simmering. Whisk ½ cup of the hot milk mixture into the cornstarch mixture to temper it.

3. Put the chocolate chips in a large heatproof bowl and pour the remaining hot milk mixture over it. Wait 30 seconds, then whisk to melt the chocolate. Add the cornstarch mixture and continue to whisk until incorporated.

4. Return the mixture to the saucepan and cook over medium-high heat, stirring continually, until it comes to a low boil and the mixture has thickened into a pudding.

5. Transfer to a large mixing bowl and, while still hot, whisk in the Nutella and butter.

6. Scoop the pudding into four serving bowls and re-frigerate for 1 hour to set up.

7. To make the crumble, preheat the oven to 350°F. Grease a baking sheet. In a mixing bowl, cream the powdered sugar and butter with a rubber spatula. Stir in the hazelnuts, flour, and salt to create a crumbly texture.

8. Transfer the crumble to the baking sheet and bake for 15–20 minutes or until golden brown and crunchy. Remove from oven and let cool. Break the crumble into smaller pieces and store in an airtight container at room temperature.

9. To make the grappa cream, combine the heavy cream and sugar in a stand mixer fitted with a wire whisk. Whip on medium speed until stiff peaks form. Add the grappa and whip for a few seconds longer. The cream can be refrigerated for up to 5 hours.

10. Right before serving, remove pudding from the refrigerator and top with crumble and a dollop of grappa cream.

CRUMBLE

⅓ cup powdered sugar

⅓ cup unsalted butter, room temperature

⅓ cup finely chopped hazelnuts

⅓ cup all-purpose flour

¼ teaspoon kosher salt

GRAPPA CREAM

1 cup heavy cream

¼ cup sugar

2 tablespoons grappa

Rainbow Cookies

These cookies are a childhood favorite. If you don't have a double boiler to melt the chocolate for this recipe, place a glass mixing bowl over a pot of simmering water.

1. Preheat the oven to 350°F. Line three 9 × 13-inch baking pans with parchment paper. Line a baking sheet with plastic wrap that is twice the width and length of the baking sheet.

2. In a stand mixer fitted with a paddle attachment, cream the almond paste, butter, sugar, and egg yolks on medium speed. With the mixer on low speed, gently add flour until thick dough forms. Remove the bowl from the mixing stand.

3. In a separate small bowl, beat the egg whites until soft peaks form. Fold egg whites into the dough using a silicone spatula.

4. Divide the dough in three equal portions. Stir red food coloring into one, green food coloring into another, and leave the third batch plain. Spread each portion into its own parchment-lined baking pan. Each layer should be about ½ inch thick.

5. Bake 10–12 minutes, or until the cake is lightly browned and a toothpick pulls clean. Invert each cake onto a cooling rack, remove parchment paper, and allow to completely cool.

MAKES 24–30 COOKIES

ACTIVE TIME = 1 HOUR

INACTIVE TIME = 8 HOURS

————————★————————

8 ounces almond paste, finely chopped

1 cup unsalted butter, room temperature

1 cup sugar

4 eggs, separated into yolks and whites

2 cups all-purpose flour

10 drops red food coloring

10 drops green food coloring

⅓ cup raspberry jam

⅓ cup apricot jam

1 cup semisweet chocolate chips

————————★————————

IF YOU DON'T HAVE THREE 9 X 13-INCH BAKING PANS, YOU CAN BAKE THE LAYERS INDIVIDUALLY.

6. Using the back of a spoon or silicone spatula, pass both jams, individually, through a fine-mesh strainer into a bowl, to remove any larger pieces and seeds. Set aside.

7. Place the green cake layer on the baking sheet lined with plastic wrap. Evenly spread raspberry jam onto the cake and top with the white layer. Evenly spread the white layer with apricot jam, and top with the red layer.

8. Pull plastic wrap up and over the layers. If it does not fully cover the top, just cover with a separate piece of plastic wrap. Place a heavy pan or cutting board on top to press the layers together. Chill in the refrigerator 8 hours or overnight.

9. Remove the cake from the refrigerator and let come to room temperature. Remove the plastic wrap.

10. Melt the chocolate chips in a double boiler, stirring until smooth. Evenly top the red layer with melted chocolate and refrigerate 1 hour.

11. Trim ⅛ inch from all edges. Slice the cake lengthwise into 1 inch strips, then slice each strip into 2 inch-wide pieces.

Stone Fruit Crostata with Spiced Mascarpone

SERVES 4–6

ACTIVE TIME = 50–55 MINUTES

———————— ★ ————————

Every year, I look forward to stone fruit season. Peaches, plums, and nectarines mean that summer is here, and I can't get enough of their juicy flesh. There's nothing like biting into a nectarine or peach and having that juice run down your chin. Mixing stone fruits in this crostata layers their flavors and brings out the best in their natural sugars.

1. Preheat oven to 350°F. Line a baking sheet with parchment paper.

2. Toast the peppercorns, allspice, and juniper berries in a dry sauté pan over medium heat for 5 minutes, shaking the pan often to prevent burning. Transfer to a spice grinder and grind into a powder.

3. In a mixing bowl, combine the fruit, sugar, and flour and toss to coat evenly. Add 1 teaspoon spice powder and toss to combine.

4. On a floured surface, roll out the pie dough to an 11-inch circle and transfer it to a parchment-lined baking sheet. Spoon the fruit mixture into the center of the dough, leaving a 2-inch border around the outside. Gently fold the edges of the dough just up over the edge of the fruit, pleating it as you go around.

5. Brush the crust with egg and dust with raw sugar. Bake 20–25 minutes, or until crust is golden brown and fruit is tender.

2 teaspoons black peppercorns

1 teaspoon ground allspice

1 teaspoon dried juniper berries

4 cups peeled and sliced stone fruit of your choice (peach, plum, apricot, nectarine)

½ cup sugar

2 tablespoons all-purpose flour

1 *Pie Dough* (recipe follows)

1 egg, beaten

1 tablespoon raw sugar

1 cup mascarpone, room temperature

2 tablespoons powdered sugar

1 cup heavy cream

ACTIVE TIME = 8–10 MINUTES

INACTIVE TIME = 1 HOUR

———————— ★ ————————

PIE DOUGH

1 stick (8 tablespoons) unsalted butter, chilled and cut into ½-inch cubes

1½ cups all-purpose flour

Pinch of kosher salt

2 tablespoons cold water

6. Combine the mascarpone, powdered sugar, and remaining spice mixture in a stand mixer fitted with a wire whisk. Whip on medium speed for 1 minute. Reduce the speed to low and slowly add the heavy cream. When all the cream has been added, increase to medium speed and whip until stiff peaks form. Refrigerate until ready to serve.

7. Remove the crostata from oven and let cool for 5 minutes before transferring to a cooling rack. Serve warm or at room temperature, topped with dollops of spiced mascarpone.

Pie Dough

1. Add the butter, flour, and salt to a food processor fitted with the plastic dough blade. Turn on the food processor and blend for approximately 15–20 seconds or until a coarse crumble forms.

2. Keeping the food processor on, add water a tablespoon at a time. The ingredients will start to pull away from the sides of the processor and a dough ball will begin to form. This will take approximately 30 seconds to 1 minute.

3. Remove the dough and form it into a ball. Wrap tightly in plastic wrap and place in the refrigerator for at least 1 hour.

Carnival-Style Zeppole with Seasonal Sugars

Every summer, the carnival came to town. They set up the rides, games, and concessions on the baseball field across the street from my house in Little Ferry, New Jersey. You could smell them heating up the oil for the zeppole in the afternoon, and it was all I could think about. Sporting a mullet and my finest Mötley Crüe T-shirt, I'd head over to the carnival to meet my friends and start the night with a brown paper bag of zeppole tossed with powdered sugar. My friends and I would walk around and try to get girls to pay attention to us—oblivious to the powdered sugar all over our black T-shirts. At the end of the night, we'd each get another bag for the walk home.

At the time, zeppole felt like a special treat: you only got to eat them one week out of the year. Now that I can make them whenever I want, I like to play around with different kinds of flavored sugar to toss them in. You can make them, too. And you don't need to break out your Guns N' Roses T-shirt to complete the experience.

SERVES 4–6

ACTIVE TIME = 45 MINUTES

———————★———————

6 cups canola oil (quantity may vary depending on your deep fryer)

1 cup water

1 stick unsalted butter

⅓ cup sugar

1½ cups all-purpose flour

4 large eggs

½ cup ricotta cheese

Zest of 1 orange

Flavored sugar (recipes follow)

1. Heat the canola oil in an electric deep fryer to 350°F. If you do not have an electric fryer, use a heavy-bottomed pot and a candy thermometer.

2. In a large saucepan, bring the water, butter, and sugar to a boil. Gently whisk in the flour. Lower the heat to low and simmer for 1 minute.

3. Transfer the mixture to the bowl of a stand mixer fitted with the paddle attachment and beat on medium speed for 2 minutes. Add the eggs one at a time, allowing one to be fully incorporated before adding the next one. Add the ricotta and orange zest, and mix on medium speed until combined. You may need to stop and scrape down the inside of the mixing bowl to ensure all the ingredients are incorporated.

4. When the oil has reached 350°F, scoop 1 tablespoon of batter and gently drop it into the oil. Fry in small batches for 5 minutes until golden brown, turning them halfway through to cook evenly. Using a wok skimmer or slotted spoon, remove the zeppole from the oil and drain on paper towels.

5. Toss with sugar of your choice and transfer to a serving dish. Serve immediately.

Spiced Sugar

2 cups sugar

1 teaspoon cinnamon powder

½ teaspoon ground allspice

¼ teaspoon ground cloves

Whisk all ingredients together to incorporate.

———————★———————

Strawberry Powder

2 cups powdered sugar

¾ cup freeze-dried strawberries

Blend sugar and strawberries in a food processor until strawberries have turned into a powder and you have pink sugar.

———————★———————

Chocolate Powder

1½ cups powdered sugar

½ cup unsweetened cocoa powder

Whisk sugar and cocoa powder together to incorporate.

menu suggestions

Many of the recipes in this book are designed to be served to four people as small plates. Below are some menu suggestions that pull together groups of recipes for different social occasions.

Date Night

Whether you've been together for years and want to set aside some time for just the two of you or you want to impress a new crush, here are four recipes you can pull off easily and set the tone for a really great night.

Baked Ricotta with Scallion, Speck, and Saba (page 68)—snack on this with a glass of wine to set the mood

Roasted Cauliflower with Pecorino and Mint (page 34)—a great complement to the main course

Veal Cutlet with Asparagus, Basil, and Lemon (page 135)—a main course that's light and flavorful

Rosemary Panna Cotta with Spiced Orange Compote and Pine Nuts (page 304)—a big-flavor dessert to wrap up your date-night meal

Entertaining

Cooking for friends is a great way to spend an evening, and having people over on a Sunday night will help chase away the Monday blues. Straighten up the living room, grab a few bottles of wine, call five or six friends, put on some good music, and let the good times roll. All these recipes have do-ahead elements, so you won't be chained to the stove all night.

Smoked Olives (page 4)—these go great with cocktails, beer, and wine

Whipped Burrata with Toast and Thyme (page 59)—look at you with your homemade cheese, you rock star

Yellowfin Tuna Crudo with Crushed Pine Nuts and Aged Balsamic (page 240)—easy, light, and so good

Scallop Cutlets with Bacon Bread Crumbs and Arugula Pesto (page 214)—full of flavor

Chicken Wings with Pepperoni Sauce (page 12)—these will surely be a hit with your friends

Nutella Cookie Sandwiches (page 296)—you might want to double the recipe for these and package some up for your friends to take home

Family Night

Taking the time to sit at the table together and talk about your day is really important to do as often as you can. Doing it over a really good meal? Even better.

Shaved Fennel with Peaches and Hazelnuts (page 30)—feel free to experiment with different fresh fruit elements in this salad

Mom's Broiled Chicken with Potatoes and Onions (page 123)—light and dark meat, broiled; an easy way to get dinner on the table

Stone Fruit Crostata with Spiced Mascarpone (page 313)—a dessert everyone in the family will love

Summer Party Time

Throwing a big outdoor party is what summer is all about. You roast the Pig in a Box with Sour Orange Relish (page 250) and make the party a

potluck—ask your friends to bring these other dishes so there are things to snack on while the pig is doin' its thing.

Pork-Fried Peanuts (page 3)

Deviled Bacon, Egg, and Cheese (page 14)

Ricotta with Charred Asparagus and Harissa Vinaigrette (page 60)

Steamed Mussels with Pancetta, Yuengling, and Goat Cheese (page 217)

Warm Octopus Salad with Potato, Kalamata Olives, and Pancetta (page 161)

Pistachio Gelato (page 295)

Honey-Soaked Cookies (page 299)

metric conversions

The recipes in this book have not been tested with metric measurements, so some variations might occur. Remember that the weight of dry ingredients varies according to the volume or density factor: 1 cup of flour weighs far less than 1 cup of sugar, and 1 tablespoon doesn't necessarily hold 3 teaspoons.

GENERAL FORMULA FOR METRIC CONVERSION

Ounces to grams	multiply ounces by 28.35
Grams to ounces	multiply ounces by 0.035
Pounds to grams	multiply pounds by 453.5
Pounds to kilograms	multiply pounds by 0.45
Cups to liters	multiply cups by 0.24
Fahrenheit to Celsius	subtract 32 from Fahrenheit temperature, multiply by 5, divide by 9
Celsius to Fahrenheit	multiply Celsius temperature by 9, divide by 5, add 32

VOLUME (LIQUID) MEASUREMENTS

1 teaspoon = ⅙ fluid ounce	= 5 milliliters	
1 tablespoon	= ½ fluid ounce	= 15 milliliters
2 tablespoons	= 1 fluid ounce	= 30 milliliters
¼ cup	= 2 fluid ounces	= 60 milliliters
⅓ cup	= 2⅔ fluid ounces	= 79 milliliters
½ cup	= 4 fluid ounces	= 118 milliliters
1 cup or ½ pint	= 8 fluid ounces	= 250 milliliters
2 cups or 1 pint	= 16 fluid ounces	= 500 milliliters
4 cups or 1 quart	= 32 fluid ounces	= 1,000 milliliters
1 gallon	= 4 liters	

WEIGHT (MASS) MEASUREMENTS

1 ounce	= 30 grams	
2 ounces	= 55 grams	
3 ounces	= 85 grams	
4 ounces	= ¼ pound	= 125 grams
8 ounces	= ½ pound	= 240 grams
12 ounces	= ¾ pound	= 375 grams
16 ounces	= 1 pound	= 454 grams

OVEN TEMPERATURE EQUIVALENTS, FAHRENHEIT (F) AND CELSIUS (C)

100°F	= 38°C
200°F	= 95°C
250°F	= 120°C
300°F	= 150°C
350°F	= 180°C
400°F	= 205°C
450°F	= 230° C

VOLUME (DRY) MEASUREMENTS

¼ teaspoon	= 1 milliliter
½ teaspoon	= 2 milliliters
¾ teaspoon	= 4 milliliters
1 teaspoon	= 5 milliliters
1 tablespoon	= 15 milliliters
¼ cup	= 59 milliliters
⅓ cup	= 79 milliliters
½ cup	= 118 milliliters
⅔ cup	= 158 milliliters
¾ cup	= 177 milliliters
1 cup	= 225 milliliters
4 cups or 1 quart	= 1 liter
½ gallon	= 2 liters
1 gallon	= 4 liters

LINEAR MEASUREMENTS

½ in	= 1½ cm
1 inch	= 2½ cm
6 inches	= 15 cm
8 inches	= 20 cm
10 inches	= 25 cm
12 inches	= 30 cm
20 inches	= 50 cm

thank you

NO CHEF ACHIEVES success on his or her own. I consider myself lucky to have been able to accomplish so many of my goals with the help of the collective and cumulative effort of my co-workers, family and friends, colleagues and mentors.

I have had the privilege of working with some pretty amazing people on this cookbook, all of whom have contributed their talents to help bring the book to life, and I couldn't be more grateful.

To my beautiful, talented wife, Stacy Isabella—thank you for your patience, love, and support. I am so appreciative for all the work you did, not just in helping me develop the recipes, but also in putting up with my crazy schedule as I continue to open new restaurants and build my business. I love you.

So much love and gratitude to my mom, Joanne, my sister, Diana, and brother, Ben, for being who they are, keeping me grounded, and supporting me every step of the way. I wouldn't be where I am today without you. Thank you.

Thank you to my agent Howard Yoon, as well as Katie McHugh, Renee Sedliar, Christine Marra, and the entire Da Capo team for making my dream of one day writing a cookbook come true.

A big thank you to two friends and collaborators: writer Carol Blymire, who "got" me from day one and whose writing so perfectly tells the stories I want to tell; and Greg Powers, a true artist, who brings my food to life through his photography.

A special thanks to Jen Resick Williams of KnowPR for being an extra set of arms, legs, eyes, and ears and an integral part of the work I do.

To my team at Graffiato: thank you for all your hard work, long hours, dedication, and focus on building the restaurant I've always dreamed of. You're all like one big crazy family to me, and I'm grateful to you all.

Thank you to the investors who believed in me, as well as my former bosses and chef mentors from whom I've learned so much over the years.

Thank you to our cookbook recipe testers: Ryan Adams, Marisa Brown, Bill and Cheryl Bunce, Catherine Gelera, Jen Grimes, Nick Hall, Aaron Keefer, Jessica Lahey, Marshall and Amy Senk, Linda Tipton, Jim Webster, and Chris Wilson.

And last, but most certainly not least: my Grandma Antoinette was and continues to be my inspiration in the kitchen, and in life. I miss you more than you could know. I hope this book would've made you proud.

about the author

MIKE ISABELLA IS the Chef/Owner of Graffiato (graffiatodc.com) and Chef/Partner of Bandolero (bandolerodc.com), and he was named *Food & Wine* magazine's The People's Best New Chef Mid-Atlantic for 2012. For the past 15 years, Chef Isabella has worked for some of the world's most renowned chefs and cooked to critical acclaim at restaurants all over the country. Before opening Graffiato, Chef Isabella was the executive chef of José Andrés' Zaytinya. During his three-year tenure, Chef Isabella generated accolades and national attention for Washington, D.C.'s Mediterranean powerhouse restaurant. His formal training began at The Restaurant School in New York, and he has worked as a sous chef for James Beard Award winner Douglas Rodriguez at Alma de Cuba in Philadelphia and as Executive Sous Chef of Marcus Samuelsson's Washington Square. In early 2013, Chef Isabella plans to open Greek restaurant, Kapnos, and Italian sandwich shop, G, both in Washington, D.C.

index

*Page references in **bold** refer to text photos.*